S0-BUW-866

SAN FRANCISCO PUBLIC LIBRARY

3 1223 904 4639

C

NEW INFORMATION TECHNOLOGIES —NEW OPPORTUNITIES

Papers presented at the 1981 Clinic on Library Applications of Data Processing, April 26-29, 1981

Clinic on Library Applications
of Data Processing: 1981

New Information Technologies —New Opportunities

Edited by
LINDA C. SMITH

Graduate School of Library and Information Science
University of Illinois at Urbana-Champaign

REF 10.78 C616p 1981

S. F. PUBLIC LIBRARY

82 -85

Library of Congress Cataloging in Publication Data

Clinic on Library Applications of Data Processing
    (18 : 1981 : University of Illinois at Urbana-
    Champaign)
    New information technologies—new opportunities.

    "Papers presented at the 1981 Clinic on
Library Applications of Data Processing, April
26-29, 1981"—Half-title p.
    Includes index.
    Contents: Introduction / Linda C. Smith —
Technology alone is not enough / Ronald L.
Wigington — The microcomputer catalyst / Howard
Fosdick — Applications of microcomputers in
libraries / Lawrence A. Woods — [etc.]
    1. Libraries—Automation—Congresses.
2. Library science—Data processing—Congresses.
3. Information storage and retrieval systems—Con-
gresses. I. Smith, Linda C. II. University of
Illinois at Urbana-Champaign. Graduate School of
Library and Information Science. III. Title.
Z678.9.C55 1981   025.3'028'54   82-10947
ISBN 0-87845-066-1

© 1982 by The Board of Trustees of The University of Illinois

CONTENTS

INTRODUCTION

The eighteenth annual Clinic on Library Applications of Data Processing was held April 26-29, 1981, at the Illini Union, University of Illinois at Urbana-Champaign. New technologies for processing, transmitting and storing information present new opportunities and challenges to libraries. The papers from the clinic discuss current developments and applications of these technologies, together with some of the issues which they raise.

Technologies for information processing include microcomputers and word processors. Fosdick presents a tutorial on microcomputers, while Woods provides many examples of microcomputer applications in technical processing, public services and management activities of libraries. Hoyt describes the many applications which the USDA's Technical Information Systems has found for the word processor. Penniman surveys available data entry and display devices.

Technologies for information transmission include videotex and teletext. Veith identifies projects in the United States and abroad which are testing the market for these new information systems. Divilbiss highlights some recent developments in telecommunications, including electronic mail, facsimile, two-way cable, and digital telephones. To store information, videodiscs now supplement the microforms and magnetic tapes with which librarians are already familiar. Schipma outlines the basic characteristics of videodiscs as a storage medium.

Complementing the papers on technology are three others which take the form of technology assessment—an analysis of some of the issues and problems raised by these technological innovations and applications. Miller addresses the question of copyright protection for computer software and databases. Nielsen explores the relationship between technological change and professional identity. In his keynote speech, Wigington cites the changing roles of the information professional as information technology evolves.

A recent book defines the "techno-peasant" as "anyone who's technologically illiterate."[1] For those who want to learn about the new information technologies, the present book offers an overview of their characteristics and potential applications.

LINDA C. SMITH
Editor

REFERENCE

1. Cunningham, Ann M., and Begley, Sharon. *The Techno-Peasant Survival Manual.* New York: Bantam Books, 1980, (cover).

RONALD L. WIGINGTON
Director of Research and Development
Chemical Abstracts Service

Technology Alone is Not Enough

Many have traced the evolution of information transfer from drawings on the walls of caves to inscriptions on stone tablets, to scribes writing on papyrus or other early forms of paper, to "Gutenberg technology." By now it has become trite to mention that computer and electronic communications together represent another revolution in the transfer and utilization of knowledge. Yet I mention it because we have only scratched the surface in understanding and using these mechanisms for supporting human learning and for facilitating human decision-making.

We are rapidly approaching the point at which the mechanical and inherent cost impediments of media and mechanisms for information transfer and knowledge production will disappear as limitations to reaching the full potential of information systems. With these impediments out of the way, what is left to inhibit knowledge creation and dissemination are the arrangements necessary to derive the revenue for supporting the information processing, distribution and use mechanisms, and, most of all, the limitations of human intelligence to deal with complex situations.

But this is getting ahead of the story. Let us first review the foundations that have been prepared for improving information handling.

Possibilities and Practicalities

I had the privilege of leading a study of the status of information technology and its application to libraries. It was done under the auspices of the National Academy of Sciences, and was supported by the Council on Library Resources. The results were published in 1972.[1]

When we entered that study, the implied question was: "Why hasn't computer technology brought the dramatic revolution to library functions that had been expected?" And, when we started, we expected to find that some underlying technology improvement was necessary for the expected improvements in library operations to occur. Yet when we finished the study, one of our conclusions was: "The primary bar to development of national level computer-based library and information systems is no longer basically a technology feasibility problem. Rather it is the combination of complex institutional and organizational human-related problems and the inadequate economic/value system associated with these activities."[2] That conclusion is even more valid today than it was in 1972.

The papers in this clinic feature several examples of new tools that are becoming widely available for a variety of information system purposes. They are very interesting and promising tools, and need to be well understood for their potential for being used in the library environment and as substitutes for functions now performed in library environments. In reading about these tools throughout these papers, one should keep in mind that they must be understood far more deeply than the obvious potential each of these tools may promise individually. The proper attitude was well stated in the November 1980 issue of *Datacomm Advisor*:

> Technology has advanced to a stage where the products and services of computer companies and the telecommunication companies are converging with those of the office equipment companies to produce information systems that can tie together dispersed information functions. The computer industry talks of distributed systems, but what we really mean are computer systems that are physically distributed but logically interconnected to respond to the information needs of an organization.[3]

This statement emphasizes that it is extremely important to understand the larger context in which the information system tools are to be applied so that they can be truly effective.

Libraries and Information Technology

Information technology is multifaceted and includes computers, telecommunications, various output devices (including photocomposers, nonimpact printers, and other image media), as well as interactive terminals. In general, information technology must provide:

—means for storage of information, appropriately organized;
—mechanisms for input of the information for machine handling;
—means for information transfer from producer to organizer, to and among storehouses, and to the consumer; also, related methods for maintenance and management of the storehouses;
—means for intellectual and physical access;

—mechanisms for output from machine form for human use;
—mechanisms for manipulation of information and for control associated with all of the above functions.[4]

Libraries, as storehouses and as institutions to enable the use of recorded human knowledge, have been around for a very long time. They are much maligned and often unappreciated institutions. Primarily because of economic pressures, they have applied technology to aid the functioning of internal library operations in acquisitions, cataloging, circulation, and interlibrary loan. Attention is now turning to improving the service-providing aspects of libraries, such as subject access and document delivery.

Toffler, in his book *The Third Wave*,[5] referred to libraries as "Second Wave" institutions based on the printed word, centralization, economy of scale, etc. He questioned how will libraries function as social memory in the future, when the information transfer medium has shifted to computer-dominated methods and there is greater decentralization and individualization in information use.

Voices for Progress

There have been many visionaries who have projected and worked toward enhanced information systems to support knowledge organization and application. Vannevar Bush, in the *Atlantic Monthly* of July 1945, described the Memex as a mechanized memory (before computers) for recording, retrieving and using knowledge in the intellectual work of individuals.[6]

Doug Engelbart, in his work of many years which led to the Laboratory for Augmentation of Human Intellect at the Stanford Research Institute, demonstrated a prototype of an "electronic Memex" and showed how to use it for a variety of purposes. It was very clear, from observing that work, that enhancement of information systems requires intellectual discipline and training in addition to automated tools. Engelbart also rediscovered the necessity for formal organization of information in the role of information center for the Advanced Research Projects Agency (ARPA) network.

J.C.R. Licklider and colleagues at the Massachusetts Institute of Technology (MIT), in the MAC system and, subsequently, the MULTICS time-shared computer system, showed that flexible computer-supported environments were effective both for computational support of science and engineering and for report production—a forerunner of modern word processing. (TYPESET and RUNOFF were programs implemented on the MIT systems which have many descendants in the present generation of word-processing systems.) Also, a farseeing, but premature, experiment in library automation, INTREX, was performed on that computer system base.

Murray Turoff of the New Jersey Institute of Technology has demonstrated in his Electronic Information Exchange System (EIES) the productive potential for a geographically and temporally dispersed interaction among individuals, and support of that interaction via organized recorded knowledge. Computer conferencing is another facet of information organization, storage and use.

F. Wilfrid Lancaster of the University of Illinois has always been a leading proponent of "paperless information systems." He has documented the implications of such systems, and library institutions would be well advised to understand those implications.

I have had the privilege of knowing all of these visionaries except Vannevar Bush, who was somewhat "before my time." What is striking, and what these researchers have in common, is that they all were unhindered by tradition and that, at one time or another, were not believed by their contemporaries.

In his National Federation of Abstracting and Indexing Service Miles Conrad Memorial Lecture in March 1980, Carlos Cuadra expressed the challenges to libraries in coping with the change in emphasis in the following way: "I do not know how well libraries will manage to shift their emphasis from a *collection* orientation to an *access* orientation, but I believe their survival depends to some extent on their success in doing this."[7] The technology tools covered in these papers are concentrated on some of the means to achieve the access orientation.

Issues and Problems

Let us turn to the issues and problems that library and information professionals must face now and in the future. These fall into four categories:

1. distributed function in an integrated environment,
2. integration of information support with the work environment,
3. the economic framework, and
4. the role of the information professional.

Distributed Function in an Integrated Environment

Several years ago, much of the focus of library automation technology attention was on the central facilities required to implement library management processes—the computers, information storage media and software for large databases, and basic teleprocessing and communication networking. In these papers, much of the attention has moved outward to the technology that will interface directly with the system users. The key elements in that technology are microcomputers of increasing power and low-cost input/output devices suitable for operation at the user site. These furnish the basis for providing functions for the user which are more responsive for small tasks than can be supported remotely over today's normal communication lines. They also provide the opportunity to support the user's own work flow directly.

These tools, however, should not be considered as isolated entities except for the most trivial jobs. Even if there were a super videodisc which would hold all the world's knowledge, its utility would have to be understood in the context of the total system necessary to collect, organize and update the information to be stored on it.

The most important functions the microcomputer technology can fulfill are to provide machine support directly to the user for coping with a heterogeneous collection of information resources, and to support the individualized interaction with that information subsequent to retrieval. Systems for online information services from library systems and from the various facets of the information industry have developed at different points in time, were guided by different design goals and principles, and are driven by different economic and service motivations. A universally standard interaction language, standard data representation, and common query formulation strategies do not exist and are not going to be developed, any more than all the countries in the world are going to switch to Esperanto. The modern Tower of Babel is embodied in the growing patchwork of resources loosely linked together by various data communication networks. Something is needed to bridge the gaps.

Intelligent terminals or, in some cases, locally supported clusters of terminals provide ways to cope with the heterogeneity and to bridge the gap between human skills and habits and the details of interacting with computer systems. Ranging from almost trivial to very challenging, the functions to be considered for implementation in such terminals include:

—automated support for administrative trivia, such as LOGON, passing of accounting and identification information, etc.;
—command language mapping and command "script" management;
—query analysis and management of the selection of resources to be accessed;
—merging and formatting of retrieved results for viewing;
—data management of, and retrieval from, private work files; and
—computer-aided training for use of all of the above-listed functions.

Until sufficiently powerful microcomputers in intelligent terminals are developed, an alternate implementation site for the more complex functions would be a service host on the network to supply such intermediary services.

Present major library "networks" are not truly computer networks. They are mostly centralized service functions reachable over public and private communication networks. Some distribution of function is beginning, but this is a relatively recent development. As one becomes serious about linking these so-called networks with each other and with other electronically accessible information services for total information support for users, the kinds of bridging functions discussed will become more necessary.

Integration of Information Support with the Work Environment

The visions of Memex will not be fully achieved until retrieval of information from formal sources (libraries and other information services) can be merged naturally with locally generated information for further use in the work flow of the information seeker. This is one of the most important needs to fill by means of distributed function, as discussed previously. In order to do this, the information must be received in the local system in digital (machine-readable) form rather than as the image of a page, or must be selectively converted from the received image by generalized OCR techniques that are not yet widely available.

Because libraries are now storehouses of printed materials, and so far only relatively small amounts of specialized materials are becoming available in computer-system-usable form from any source, there will long be a document delivery image interface for information users who must summarize, extract and rekey those aspects that are to be reused in their work. Nevertheless, library and information service delivery systems should take into account the evolving work environment of those they serve.

The Economic Framework

Despite what is becoming technologically feasible, the economic framework for information services remains in an early stage of development. As it relates to libraries, the economic framework still rests mostly on the mechanisms of the pre-photocopy publication industry and institutional funding of library services.

There have been changes, of course. New copyright laws have been passed, and attempts have been made to define the impacts of new technology. "Fee-for-service" practices have been instituted which depend on use-oriented metrics, such as "first-time use" charge of OCLC, and some net-lending libraries are charging a fee for interlibrary loan. However, the institutional funding mechanisms of governmental authorities at various levels still cope much better with fixed annual fees rather than fees based on use level. Although many industrial laboratories continue to regard their library support as part of fixed budget overhead, some treat library functions as charge-back services of value related to the direct effort of doing work. (The costs of information functions *should* be regarded in the same category as the cost of equipment for laboratory investigations.) The software industry has pioneered pricing and conditions-of-use terms that are based on the *use* of the software, rather than on the physical means of transfer of the software and the work necessary to install and maintain it.

Nevertheless, there remain issues in the economic framework that are not yet adequately settled. Contractual agreements for the access to and reuse of information, following the software marketing practices, theoretically would be able to cover any definable condition. However, we have not yet been able to cope with the transfer of retrieved information to local support systems for reuse, an important capability from the user's point of view. The boundaries of control and compensation for derivative files, especially if they come from multiple sources, remain a source of controversy between database suppliers and service vendors.

Also, information flow across national boundaries, as an item of commerce, is being subjected to the same protectionist trade policies as other goods of commerce. The communication tariffs imposed by foreign PTT (postal, telephone and telegraph authorities), which are usually governmental bodies outside the United States, are the equivalent of trade barriers for other (e.g., automobile and electronic equipment) industries. The U.S. information industry is at a disadvantage because of them.

But perhaps the most immediate economic problem facing libraries is the economy of resource sharing. The cost squeeze of the 1960s—continuing today—forced libraries to find ways to eliminate duplicative work. The initial existence of OCLC and its meteoric rise were based entirely on the advantages of resource sharing for shared cataloging.

Today, other economic facets are entering the library network picture. Some of these have different effects. To the extent that duplicative work, developmental or operational, is eliminated, resource sharing continues to be beneficial to the total society of information producers, organizers, storehouses, and especially users, by reducing the total expense of providing a specific level and range of services to users and thus reducing the total cost to the funding sources (both institutional and market-based). But to the extent that the resource-sharing actions simply redistribute the total cost of providing the information services over the total population, they are self-destructive.

This situation is best illustrated by an old story, called the "Tragedy of the Commons" and first described by William Forster Lloyd in 1833.[8] The tragedy of the commons is depicted by a pasture open to all. Each herdsman attempts to maximize the number of cattle in his herd as a hedge against the ravages of tribal wars, poaching and disease. However, as time goes on, conditions change. More social stability is achieved, reducing tribal wars and poaching, and progress is made in conquering disease. The total number of cattle of all the herdsmen reaches the total carrying capacity of the common land. As a rational being (which of course every good manager is) each herdsman seeks to maximize his gain. He is guided by principles of utility. For example, he asks, "What is the utility *to me* of adding one more animal to my herd?" The positive return is the proceeds from the sale of the added animal. There is a negative impact, also because the added animal causes overgrazing to occur, and thus reduces the efficiency of fattening for market all the animals in all the herds. However, the herdsman who added the extra animal only bears the burden of a fraction of that disadvantage, so it is still to his own advantage to add the animal. He and all the other "rational" herdsmen continue to add animal after animal, each to maximize his own return, until total ruin is reached; the overgrazing of the pastures goes beyond the limits of survival. The pasture dies, and all the herds are wiped out.

The destructive aspect of resource sharing in the library community— that part which shifts costs rather than totally eliminating them—is the equivalent of the above story. The urge is to minimize the cost of operation of each party (i.e., maximizing individual return), and the eventual result will be the wiping out of the total revenue support base necessary to supply the very substance of existence—a classic case of "killing the goose that laid the golden egg," otherwise known as suboptimization. The economic dynamics are the same, and ruin is the inevitable result. Clearly, joint economic planning and "statesmanship" are called for. Establishment of incentives to cause this to happen is one unsolved problem.

The Role of the Information Professional

Research libraries and information service intermediaries should look forward with enthusiasm to changes in their roles as library and information technology evolves. Job enrichment should result as the information professional expands into substantive work and decision-making, not remaining merely as an efficient conduit for information on the basis of which others make decisions and take actions.

The argument about "end users" versus information intermediaries as a target for the design of information service delivery system is pointless and nonproductive. More and more people who are not deeply trained in the intricacies of interaction with library and information systems will need to use computer-based systems, just as they have used card catalogs and indexes and other information location tools for many years. It was recently reported that more than 50 percent of the use of the New York Times Information Bank had already shifted to end users, rather than be used mostly by librarians or other information professionals.

The demands of the system requirements for such purposes were brought home directly to me by my daughter's frustration as a student in using the library system at Ohio State University. It is a well-established computerized catalog and circulation support system from which I get excellent service (via my local reference librarian!).

There will not be enough information professionals to handle the bulk of the interfaces with library and information systems of the future. The systems we design and operate must accommodate both classes of use. I see the important expanded roles of information professionals as these:

1. Through the understanding of information organization and retrieval principles and processes, the information professional will fill a prime role in the design of man-machine dialogue and algorithms for use by persons less experienced in information system intricacies. This elevates the attention and efforts of the information professional to the meta-level, a higher intellectual pursuit than simply personal proficiency in organizing and finding information. However, to do this, the professional can not think just about what he does well personally. He must develop a deeper understanding of processes that can be used successfully by those less highly trained.

2. Performing the very difficult information retrieval tasks for poorly formed questions and for investigations that require capabilities at the limits of those available from established service systems will still require the attention of the experienced information professional. For example, an experienced stock car driver can safely get far more performance out of an automobile than can the general population of drivers.

3. Expansion into performing interpretative studies, including studies requiring subject expertise beyond that of information system skills, is another direction for enrichment. Studies performed by the Congressional Research Service for members of Congress and the many interpretative reports for business planning, financial management and technology applications that are being marketed are two examples. As our society becomes more and more an information-dominated one, these functions will be needed more universally, and the persons who perform them must have dual competence—subject and information mechanics.

Conclusion

I hope that these remarks cause you to think about the multifaceted issues and impacts you face as library and information professionals. Our activities are crucial in the effective functioning of modern society, which is very dependent on effective utilization of past knowledge as a support base for present understanding, innovation and decision-making. We are called upon to make effective use of technology toward those ends.

REFERENCES

1. Information Systems Panel, Computer Science and Engineering Board. *Libraries and Information Technology: A National System Challenge*. Washington, D.C.: National Academy of Sciences, 1972.

2. Ibid., p. iv.

3. "Honeywell Announces Distributed Systems Architecture." *Datacomm Advisor* 4(Nov. 1980):1.

4. Information Systems Panel, *Libraries and Information Technology*, p. 65.

5. Toffler, Alvin. *The Third Wave*. New York: William Morrow, 1980.

6. Bush, Vannevar. "As We May Think." *Atlantic Monthly* 176(July 1945):101-08.

7. Cuadra, Carlos. "Surviving the Eighties: New Roles for Publishers, Information Science Organizations, and Users." *NFAIS Newsletter* 22(April 1980):34.

8. *See* Hardin, Garrett. "The 'Tragedy of the Commons.' " *Science* 162(13 Dec. 1968):1243-48.

HOWARD FOSDICK
Independent Computer Consultant

The Microcomputer Catalyst

Introduction

Microcomputer—it is a word many of us first heard only a couple of years ago. Yet the technology this word represents holds promise of tremendous change. The changes catalyzed by microcomputing and its associated technologies may alter the fundamental nature of information handling in all its forms. This, of course, means that libraries and information centers will be profoundly affected by this new technology. This paper attempts to indicate some possible directions of the changes prompted by microcomputing technology. However, these ideas are offered only with the disclaimer that technology in this area is developing so rapidly that no one involved in computing can fully understand its implications. Hardware designers and software engineers involved in microcomputing are themselves still attempting to discern the values and possible uses of microcomputers. The only "given" most would agree upon is the recognition that microcomputers will alter the basic manner in which computers are used and viewed in our society.

General Definitions

Before exploring the implications of the previous statements in relation to information processing, some basic definition of *microcomputer* needs to be established. This task is, unfortunately, much more difficult than it first appears. Most of us presently conceive of micrcomputers as computers physically small enough to be called "desk-top" computers. This definition is readily usable, if not always strictly accurate. Another nontechnical definition would state that a microcomputer is a computer one can purchase at a retail store. This would include, for example, the Radio Shack or Apple computers, widely advertised on television. This definition is fine, too, so long as it is recognized that this expresses only one aspect of microcomputing. The concept of retail outlets for microcomputers has developed only in the past few years, and it should be borne in mind that microcomputers themselves were only invented in 1974 or 1975. So the methods of microcomputer sales and distribution are recent phenomena that may be subject to change. Furthermore, this last definition underplays the vast usage of microcomputers in business and industry, as well as the sale and distribution of these computers through "traditional" computer hardware vendors in a manner similar to the sale and servicing of the larger mainframe or minicomputers.

A Hardware Definition

Another approach to a definition of *microcomputer* can be derived from the technology on which computers are based. The invention of the "microprocesser" by Intel introduced microtechnology in 1971. A microprocesser (MPU) is a dense package of electrical circuitry etched on a piece of silicon typically smaller than a common postage stamp. The essential characteristic of the MPU is that it has the ability to perform the operations of its instruction set. Hence, the MPU can be a processer in the same sense as the central processer unit at the heart of any minicomputer or mainframe. However, at only several dollars per MPU, this technology represents a vastly cheaper form of central processer than was previously available.

It appears quite likely that MPUs will become integrated into a vast array of consumer products in "process control" or "product-specific intelligence" functions. In fact, MPUs already provide intelligence in products ranging from automobiles to microwave ovens and washer/dryers. This paper will not concern itself with these dedicated applications of MPUs, but rather with microcomputers. The difference between the two is simply that the microcomputer represents the addition of other components necessary for the creation of a full-fledged general-purpose computer. (For example, a microcomputer must include internal memory capability. In microcomputers, this memory presently is also based on microchip technology—silicon chips manufactured in a manner very similar to that of the processing unit itself.) A microcomputer must be programmable, and it is, therefore, a general-purpose computer.

A "microcomputing system" connotes the addition of associated hardware to the microcomputer. Storage devices provide the system with mass storage or external storage capability. In large computer systems, magnetic tapes and discs provide this capability. Microcomputer systems have analogous kinds of magnetic storage media. Floppy discs were invented concurrently with microcomputers and represent one common form of storage for those systems. Floppy discs are small discs, usually measuring either (approximately) five or eight inches in diameter. These discs have storage capacities commonly measured in terms of hundreds of thousands of characters (where about a thousand characters is called a kilobyte), or in millions of characters (megabytes). The storage capacity provided by any particular manufacturer depends on that vendor's hardware specifications. Various forms of tapes are also in widespread use in microcomputer systems. Cassette tapes, exactly the same as those used in home tape recorders, have been used. More sophisticated tape systems, similar to those on larger computers, are also available. Other forms of external storage exist, as well. Punched paper tape was popular on early systems, but its use has faded before the durability and recording density of magnetic tapes. Hard disc systems, like those of minicomputers, are a most significant form of magnetic media for microcomputers. Introduced in the late 1970s, these typically offer greater storage capacities than is possible with floppy discs, but the hard disc surfaces are not removable as with floppy technology. For many industrial and library applications, hard discs have quickly become a standard storage peripheral.

For output, printers commonly come in two primary varieties: dot matrix and impact. The dot matrix printers tend to be faster and less expensive, but the print quality varies. Impact printers, such as the "daisy-wheel" printers, offer letter-quality output. But these are comparatively slow and expensive. An extremely competitive situation has developed among firms attempting to design the first low-cost printers offering both speed and word-processing quality. At the time of this writing, the first letter-quality dot matrix printers are appearing on the market. These printers achieve high print quality by techniques such as dot overlapping and multiple-pass over-printing.

Finally, in characterizing the hardware nature of microcomputer systems, it is important to recognize the online orientation of such systems. The computer terminal, or CRT with keyboard, is the predominant means of interaction with microcomputers. Microcomputer systems have skipped the batch-orientation phase of development evident in the evolution of mainframe systems.

MPU Architectures

The various kinds of hardware commonly associated with microcomputer technology having briefly been mentioned, it is appropriate to discuss further the microprocesser units themselves. Until about 1980, the vast majority of general-purpose microcomputers employed processers with 8-bit word sizes. This means that the instruction set was designed such that the basic unit of information manipulated by the computer was one "byte" (eight bits of information). Three major groups of microprocesser architectures, or "families," established dominance. These microprocesser families are the 8080/Z80, the 6800, and the 6502.

Although microcomputer sales still emphasized 8-bit MPU architecture as of late 1980, the emphasis in microprocesser *design* has definitely shifted toward 16-bit and 32-bit architectures. The 16-bit microprocessers descended from the 8080/Z80 8-bit family include the 8086 and the Z8000. Motorola's 68000 represents the 16-bit evolution of the 6800, while the 16-bit descendant of the 6502 is still a rumor, called the 6516, at the time of this writing. The first 32-bit microprocessers were publicly demonstrated in early 1981. These include the iAPX 432 from Intel, and others from Hewlett-Packard. IBM is said to have a microprocesser utilizing the Series 360 instruction set in a working prototype stage.

There are several reasons for this evolution of microprocesser architecture toward 16- and 32-bit designs. The first is that the 8-bit microcomputers of the 1975-80 era were architecturally limited to maximum internal memory sizes of 64 kilobytes. This is not much of a problem for many personal computers, but it can be a severe limitation on a business or industrially-oriented computer system. Sixteen- and 32-bit MPU designs represent one remedy to this limitation. Second, most minicomputers have 16-bit words, while mainframes most often have 32-bit designs. Thus, creation of microcomputers of these word sizes raises the distinct possibility of various degrees of software compatibility among microcomputers, minicomputers and mainframes. In essence, microtechnology could become just another hardware technique in building what were once considered minicomputers and mainframes. The implications of this idea will be more thoroughly explored later in this paper.

Microcomputer Software

From a computer systems viewpoint, the software, or programs, run on any computer are as important as the hardware itself. Most microcomputers are purchased with various essential software packages. The software may be either included as part of the basic microcomputer-system price, or priced separately for the user to buy as an option. In either case, almost any use of a microcomputer (except for very limited or special-purpose uses) requires certain essential software. Among these programs are: (1) an operating system, which is a basic control program that monitors operation and use of the computer system; (2) various programming languages, which are used in the development of computer programs; (3) text editors, or word processing software, which facilitate the creation and manipulation of textual products (e.g., correspondence or this paper); (4) networking or telecommunications software, which makes it possible to have the microcomputer communicate with other microcomputers or computing systems; and (5) general-purpose utility programs, which perform common tasks for the user (e.g., making backup copies of programs or data).

This list has included only a few of the many kinds of programs available for microcomputer systems. They are all "systems programs," or programming products with which, or upon which, the user's "applications programs" are built. The applications programs are the programs that are created to handle a particular need of the end user. For example, a library circulation program is an application program that fulfills an end user need. Needless to say, as the microcomputer market matures, applications-program products are increasingly being offered for sale for microcomputer systems.

One important trend in computing has been the evolution of the "turnkey" system approach. In this approach, the applications programs required by the end user or purchaser of the computer system are provided by the vendor of the system with the system hardware. The previous example of a library circulation system is pertinent to this concept. A library could purchase a microcomputer system, along with some of the basic systems programs mentioned earlier, and then create its own circulation system applications program(s). Or, it might be possible for the library to purchase an existing or generalized circulation program and avoid some of the costs associated with creating that software itself. In the case of the turnkey system, the necessary applications software is obtained with the hardware directly from one fully responsible vendor. The vendor must provide the computer programs and ensure they operate correctly. This approach has been widely used with circulation systems and minicomputer technology. The principle has been belabored here because the economics of microcomputing technology are such that the turnkey approach may become widely popular with microcomputing systems. This is especially true in that microcomputers are inexpensive enough that they can be economically dedicated to special-purpose or single-purpose applications. In view of microcomputer hardware costs, it is quite realistic to speak of having one turnkey microcomputer system dedicated to one library function, with other microcomputer system(s) dedicated to other computing needs.

Trends in Computer Hardware Costs

In the previous sections, the present characteristics of microcomputer hardware and software have been briefly discussed. It should be kept in mind, however, that the pace of change in this field is unbelievably rapid, and that change itself is an aspect of central importance in considering microcomputer systems. For this reason, I will offer speculation on a few of the directions microtechnology may take; but first, it is appropriate to place the impact of microtechnology in perspective by providing an analysis of historical trends in computing costs. The sketches in figure 1 are rough approximations only, but they serve to tell a significant story.

The first few graphs indicate that the relative prices of major computer hardware components have been dropping since the inception of computers. These major components of computing systems include the "main memory" or "internal memory" of the computer, as well as the "external" or "mass" storage represented by magnetic storage media like tape and disc.

Whether or not the price/performance ratio decreases were constant, and the exact figures involved, is not important for the purposes of comparison. The important point is contained in figure 1b. This diagram shows that the historical decline in central processor prices has not participated in the general hardware price decline to the extent of other computing system components. Even with the introduction of minicomputers in the late 1960s, processors remained somewhat dear. The essential impact of the microprocesser is that it has drastically bent this last curve during the past five or eight years. The fundamental price equation of computing has been altered in a dramatic way—for the first time in history, processors themselves have led the price/performance revolution. For example, the computing power one can purchase in an MPU like Intel's 8080 for $4 today cost approximately $500,000 in 1969.[1] Computing intelligence itself is now being distributed on a massive scale.

Possible Impacts

By isolating the essential fact that intelligence (the central processing unit) has recently become very inexpensive, many of the possible impacts of microtechnology become clearer. The fundamental nature of computing itself will be affected by this new cost reality concerning processors. For example, in order to gain processing efficiencies, mainframe computer systems have long exhibited a hierarchical scheme of intelligence. In the center of the system was the single central processer unit. Around this unique resource, a hierarchy of lesser special-purpose processors was arranged. Peripheral intelligences, including channels, control units and controllers, offered the central processer the opportunity to off-load a certain amount of its work to these special-purpose, limited processers. But now, with the introduction of MPUs and microcomputers, fully intelligent, more flexible processers are available in abundance. Why have a

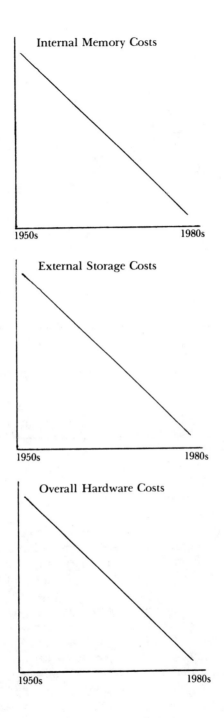

Fig. 1a. Trends in Computer Hardware Costs

Central Processer Unit (CPU) Costs

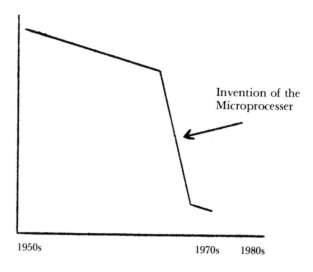

Fig. 1b. Trends in Central Processer Costs

channel, with its limited instruction set, when a more programmable and flexible MPU will cost-effectively fill the same role? I am not necessarily advocating the replacement of channels with MPUs—there are many more technical aspects of such a decision which need not be explored in this paper. The essential point is that microcomputers offer a potential in the design and implementation of large systems that just did not exist before the MPU revolution.

Other, related possible impacts are those of "front-end" and "back-end" processers. "Front-end" processers are computers dedicated to handling communications, as in a mainframe system, for example. "Back-end" processers represent the similar attempt to off-load database processing. Needless to say, inexpensive microcomputer systems may make both these technologies of mainframe design ever more affordable. Most interestingly, microcomputers are so inexpensive that they can be utilized as dedicated "front-ends" or "back-ends" to minicomputers, or even other microcomputers. Again, we do not need to delve into technological specifics to see that microcomputers can have a fundamental impact on computer systems design in this area.

The previous suggestions concerning possible impacts of microcomputer technology have been related to the manner in which microcomputers may affect traditional or preexisting mainframe design approaches.

Such possibilities represent a very basic alteration of the manner in which general-purpose computers can be designed. It would, however, be presumptuous—and almost certainly inaccurate—to limit our view of microcomputers to the ways in which they fit into mainframe design structures. For example, some microcomputer proponents have advocated creation of a computer with mainframe power through groups of full-fledged microcomputer systems closely interconnected by software methodologies. The IMSAI Hypercube is an example of one such attempt to tie microcomputers closely together into software configurations whose aggregate power can compete with mainframes. There are several variations and approaches to implementation of this idea of creating the processing power of a mainframe from a collection of software-interwoven microcomputers. Since the software involved would be sophisticated, such systems will take time to develop, but further experimentation and progress on this theme is certain.

A somewhat related idea is that of the microcomputer network. This concept advocates creation of micro-nets with large aggregate computing power, such as already discussed. However, the emphasis is not on "aggregate power" (a mainframe replacement approach), but rather on the expandability and flexibility offered by microcomputer networks. For example, current "local network" products, such as Zilog's Z-Net, Nestar System's Cluster/One, and Corvus System's Constellation, promote flexibility in network-wide resource sharing. Expansion of the network is natural and convenient, in that one need only add another (compatible) microcomputer. This is in contrast to a minicomputer, for example, where addition of another (dumb) terminal means less power, not more. Traditional minicomputer and mainframe systems configurations can be enhanced only by adding computational power at the center.

In the discussion of MPU families, the migration of MPUs toward 16- and 32-bit architectures was briefly mentioned. This raises the probability that many computers which are today considered minicomputers or mainframes could be built using microtechnology. In fact, several companies have already announced 32-bit MPUs that are clearly intended to evolve into what are being called "micromainframes." In terms of traditional computing, the impacts of this trend could be enormous. An especially intriguing idea related to the micromainframe concept is the possibility of a "370 on a chip." It appears quite possible to create an MPU having the instruction set of the widespread 360/370/4300/303X/3081 series of mainframe computers from IBM on a single microchip. At the time of this writing, it is said that IBM has already accomplished this development.

The possible significance of such a microcomputer mainframe is that the vast universe of software currently available for the 370 family of computers would be instantly accessible. Since the mid-1960s, this computer family and its relations have totally dominated mainframe sales. More programmers are familiar with it than any other general-purpose mainframe, and more software has been created for it than for any other mainframe. At the present time, it is widely agreed that the creation of software of adequate quality, in a reasonable time and for a reasonable cost, is the major problem facing any computer-using organization. This problem has become so serious, it is often referred to as the "software problem." The realization of a "plug-compatible replacement" for a 370-class mainframe through MPU technology could lead to a much greater proliferation of the computer system best positioned to reduce the software problem through existing programming.

The desirability of 32-bit micromainframes of "plug-compatible"—or "code-compatible"—design is not universally acknowledged, however. Some people feel that 370 compatibility is inimical to the basic software simplicity offered in microcomputer-based systems. Others state that microtechnology can best be utilized in new computer designs that do not imitate the computer architectures of the past. For example, some MPU designers feel that the true promise of the technology in attacking the "software problem" lies in using this inexpensive intelligence to move some traditional areas of software concern into the hardware. For example, processers could be dedicated to particular software functions, such as system memory management or programming-language interpretation. Whatever approaches are taken concerning these questions, the implications of micromainframes of one kind or another are sure to be important in terms of current business uses of computers.

The development of "viewdata" and "teletext"-type systems represents another major possible application of microcomputer technology. Clearly, these systems will have an expanding need for intelligence to facilitate and control their services. As such systems evolve and grow, microcomputers will offer a significant, perhaps vital, technology for expansion. For example, where a truly mass market is implied, microprocesser/microcomputer intelligence in the television (the entry-point terminal to the system) appears likely. This would give the end user of such a system local computing power while avoiding excessive telecommunications costs. Thus, the use of microcomputers would appear to offer the designers of these systems one possible method of allowing the necessary aggregate computing power in the systems to expand naturally in response to growth of the total user base.

As stand-alone systems, microcomputers can be put to dozens of uses in libraries. I have not explored their uses in this respect, because they are far too numerous to discuss in a single paper. As significant as the concept of the microcomputer as a stand-alone system, however, is the impetus micro-technology has given to the decentralization of computing. That is, the trend in computing from the mid-1960s through the early 1970s was widely viewed as one of centralization. Large computer systems became increasingly powerful, and even with the advent of the minicomputer, much of the attention in computing was focused on the evolution of these large computer centers. In the mid- and late 1970s, however, the microcomputer entered the picture. The vast cost reductions of semiconductor technology in terms of memory and MPU intelligence led to the ascendancy of the "distributed processing" concept. With inexpensive intelligence available, it could now be applied in "distributed systems," essentially closely interwoven networks of computer resources. Processers themselves, once so dear, would be a common resource within the distributed processing scheme. As networking and communications software are developed, we can expect to see microcomputers having impacts far beyond those immediately apparent in their uses in dedicated and stand-alone systems.

Conclusion

In this discussion, only a few of the many impacts microcomputing is likely to have on the basic nature of computing have been mentioned. Clearly, it lies beyond the scope of a single paper to do much more than suggest a few of the present and future impacts and uses of microcomputers. But from this confusion of possibilities, two facts emerge most distinctly. The first is that microcomputers will change the fundamental nature of computing in ways that cannot yet be fathomed. One should not restrict one's views of microcomputing to limited or preconceived notions, nor should one blithely assume that the present impacts of microcomputers foreshadow or determine their future uses. Second, each of us should be fully and consciously aware of the unbelievable rate of change and development in this area. Such change is itself a major aspect of microcomputing, and it must be considered and included in any plan or outlook pertaining to the use of microcomputing technology.

For Further Information

In the space of the past five years of microtechnological hardware development, several technologies related to microcomputers have already risen and fallen in importance and usage. For example, punched paper tape has already reached near-obsolescence as a storage medium, while microcomputer hard disc capabilities and 16-bit processors, both introduced about 1978, are becoming standard in many industrial systems. And computer technologies such as optical disc loom as potentially prominent in the future.

With the pace of microcomputer hardware development so unbelievably rapid, a paper such as this is truly outdated the moment it is published. Furthermore, it can be simply misleading after several years. For this reason, a list of current microcomputer journals and newspapers has been included as appendix A. The reader is cautioned that only very recent issues of these computer magazines and newspapers will provide current information concerning the state of the art in microcomputer hardware, software and pricing. Books are useful for background information and concepts concerning microcomputers, but the time lag inevitably involved in their publication prevents them from providing current hardware and software specifications. With this caution, a brief listing of sources for further information on microcomputers follows in appendix B.

ACKNOWLEDGMENTS

The author wishes to thank the following persons at GTE AE Laboratories for their constructive criticisms of this paper: Dennis Beckley, Ed Moran, Dave Smart, and Mason Wright. Also, thanks are expressed to Priscilla Polk of Automated Concepts Incorporated.

APPENDIX A

Microcomputer Magazines and Newspapers

Key: B = Of likely interest to persons beginning in microcomputers; or, particularly oriented toward the hobbyist market.

M = Of medium difficulty/readability. May be of interest to persons from neophytes to professionals.

P = Oriented toward, or most useful to, computer professionals; or, requiring substantial technical background or training.

Byte (M)
—articles on hardware & software, widely popular

Computer Design (P)
—computer electronics

Computerworld (M)
—general computing news, special section on mini's & micro's

Creative Computing (B)
—game orientation, hobbyist market

Disk/Trend Report (P)
—current news on hardware advances useful to industry insiders

Dr. Dobb's Journal of Computer Calisthenics and Orthodontia (M)
—has published some of the more widely recognized articles

Electronic Design (P)
—a weekly magazine on computer electronics

Electronic Engineering Times (P)
—weekly newspaper for microcomputer hardware professionals

IEEE Micro (P)
—new technical microcomputer publication from the IEEE

Infoworld (M)
—perhaps the best single news source for software professionals

Interface Age (M)
—similar to *Byte*, has a wide coverage, esp. for small businesses

Microsystems (M)
—new source devoted to S-100 and CP/M systems

Mini-Micro Computer Reports (P)
—up-to-the-minute news in the mini/micro industry

Mini-Micro Systems (M)
—excellent overview articles and product surveys, also tutorials

onComputing (M)
—quarterly with many nice articles for micro enthusiasts

Personal Computing (B)
—another of the popular magazines on personal computers

Random Access International (P)
—expensive information on new hardware for industry insiders

Recreational Computing (B)
—describes interesting applications, oriented toward hobbyists

Appendix A—*Continued*

Silicon Gulch Gazette (B)
  —gossip and news from the valley, news on new micro applications
Small Business Computers Magazine (M)
  —oriented toward common business uses of microcomputers
Small Systems World (M)
  —particularly good for tutorials for mini- and micro-software

APPENDIX B

Sources for Microcomputer Information

Clubs—
  A wide variety of microcomputer clubs exists, ranging from local to national organizations. Some consist purely of local hobbyists, whereas others are "official" product or company user groups. Clubs are an excellent source of information from experienced users concerning specific hardware and software products.

Newsletters—
  A myriad of microcomputer newsletters address the needs of user groups of particular hardware and/or software. Many also serve as organs for either independent or partisan clubs and vendors. Newsletters are most often special-interest in their orientations.

Computer consultants—
  In the business world, computing talent is not inexpensive. But, a system proposal or programming project of large size or sophistication may well present a need for professional consultants or a permanent professional staff. Advertisements in the magazines and newspapers enumerated in Appendix A are one source of consultant listings.

Conferences/shows—
  Personal computer shows as well as microcomputer exhibits at traditional computer conventions provide an excellent chance to meet hardware manufacturers, software vendors, large retailers and interesting and creative individuals all under one roof. There are now dozens of such shows of national and local import; two of the best known are the West Coast Computer Faire, and the National Computer Conference (NCC).

Books—
  Hardback and softbound books are available on almost any aspect of microcomputing, from programming through advanced hardware internals. In general, books are best for learning fundamentals and principles.

Retail stores—
  The burgeoning growth of microcomputer retail outlets has resulted in another major source of information for microcomputer users. Local store owners can provide names of clubs, newsletters and other organizations pertinent to microcomputing in their locale.

Appendix B—*Continued*

Magazines—

Newspapers and magazines devoted to microcomputing are perhaps the best sources for current information in printed form. This is as opposed to: (1) books, and (2) articles in library journals. (These sources generally suffer from publication lead times that are unreasonable in terms of microcomputer evolution.) Since periodicals are so vital, a list of some of the major ones is provided here. Some indication as to the general readability and orientations of the magazines is given by the associated key. This key should not be taken literally—it is only the author's casual opinion and is intended simply as an initial guide in information-seeking.

REFERENCE

1. *Datamation*, vol. 27, no. 2, Feb. 1981, p. 56.

LAWRENCE A. WOODS
Head, Research and Development
Purdue University Libraries

Applications of Microcomputers in Libraries

Five years ago it was predicted that microcomputers would take the library world by storm. As a matter of fact, this has not happened. Rather, there has been a steady, but quiet, grassroots movement introducing microcomputers not only into traditional areas of library automation, but into areas that previously have had only minimal impact from the electronic revolution.

There are four basic reasons for the slowness in developing library applications on microcomputers. The most important of these is the storage limitation at this stage of microtechnology. Systems people think in terms of kilobytes or megabytes of storage. Libraries are apt to think in terms of the number of characters in a MARC record or in a page of text 8½ by 11 inches. A kilobyte is 1000 characters, or about 2 MARC records. A megabyte is 1 million characters, or about 2000 MARC records. Similarly, a page of text 8½ by 11 inches is about 2 kilobytes, and a megabyte is about 500 pages of text. A typical microcomputer will have 32 or 64 kilobytes of main memory, and perhaps up to a megabyte of floppy disc storage, which could hold around 2000 MARC records. The present upper limit of hard disc storage for microcomputers is around 60 megabytes, which translates into 120,000 MARC records or 30,000 pages of text. Storage technology is changing rapidly and will not be a limiting factor within five to ten years.

A second limitation of microcomputers is the amount of space in which to run a program; this is called "core" in computer jargon. On a larger machine, someone with limited knowledge of programming eventually can make a program work. A microcomputer is not forgiving of inefficient programming. Often a program has to be written on a larger computer, compiled, and then read into the microcomputer. This is called "downloading."

A third factor that has hindered microcomputers from becoming widely used in libraries is the very success of microtechnology. The rate of change of technical breakthroughs has been so rapid that software producers have been reluctant to put large amounts of software development capital into a given state of technology which may be outdated in a couple of years.

Finally, software resource sharing has been minimal in the field. Because of their very nature, microcomputer applications have had a relatively low profile. The cost of the hardware is a small line item in most library budgets. The applications themselves have been largely back-room operations, and no good medium for software exchange has been developed. This problem is being remedied by the publication of several newsletters focusing on the use of microcomputers in libraries, and at least two monographs are being prepared on microcomputers in libraries.

Before proceeding with this discussion, let us look again at the definition of *microcomputer*. Some have defined it as a computer that has 4-bit "word" boundaries, or even 8-bit "word" boundaries. As a matter of fact, 16- and 32-bit microcomputers are becoming widely used. Phsyical size has been another qualifier. In fact, the term *desk-top computer* has come into vogue in some circles. Still another qualifier that has been used is price, using the figures $10,000 or $25,000 as an artificial boundary. For this paper, any machine using a microchip-based central processing unit (CPU) is a microcomputer. They range from 4-bit to 32-bit machines, and vary in price from $800 to $50,000 for a system.

One final disclaimer must be offered. This presentation is taken from work in progress on a monograph to be published by Knowledge Industry Publications and on a SPEC kit for the Association of Research Libraries Office of Management Studies. Some of the applications have not been thoroughly checked, and most have not been evaluated. The applications have been organized into four broad categories: technical processing, public services, management, and a category so broad I have called it "other."

Technical Processing

Acquisitions

Acquisitions is an area that has been slow to be automated. A fully automated acquisition system requires a complex interaction among several data files, and ought to be a data acquisitions system for the library's bibliographic files as well as a materials acquisition system. Several limited acquisition systems have been written on microcomputers.

An early attempt was the order printing system written by Richard Anable at SUNY-Binghamton on an Apple microcomputer. Related programs produced mailing labels from a vendor file and generated claim letters on request.

More recently, an expanded system was written on a Radio Shack TRS-80 I for the Glendora (California) Public Library by its director, John Jolly. He used ROM Level II Basic and a disc-operating system from Radio Shack called "Apparative." The TRS-80 I model has 48k of main memory and uses two 75k disc drives. The system is rounded out with a Qume Printer and a TRS-80 Line Printer III. The system accepts acquisitions data and prints the order forms, retaining the records on a disc file. Update, receipt and cancellation programs all access the online database. An in-process list is generated which tracks each item from date of order to two months after receipt. The vendor file has online update capability. Other programs running on the microcomputer include a list of city employees with salary, benefits and personnel management information. This program more than justified to the city the purchase of the TRS-80 I for the library.

A similar system was written for a larger microcomputer at Imperial Chemical Industries (ICI) in Great Britain. The ICI system was written on a Jacquard J-500, which has 128k of main memory and uses 250k discs. The software was written in ten days by a professional programmer.[1]

A still more complex system was written for the National Library of Medicine (NLM). The Integrated Library System (ILS) was written to run on several machines including an LSI 11/23, one of the larger microcomputers developed by Digital Equipment Corporation (DEC). A typical configuration to run the software includes the microcomputer, a video terminal, a printer, and disc storage of about 64 megabytes, costing around $50,000. It can be expanded to 4 CRTs, 256 megabytes, and has an online interface to an OCLC terminal. The software is written in MIIS/MUMPS and, since the project was federally sponsored, is available under a license from the National Technical Information Service (NTIS).

Another acquisition system currently under development is being written by John Blair at Texas A&M Medical Sciences Library. The system will run on five interlinked Micromation computers. In addition to acquisitions, it will handle the general accounting for the College of Medicine. A project is also underway to allow remote users to communicate with the reference desk by electronic mail to transmit materials requests and reference questions and to receive research results. A microwave link will replace traditional telephone lines.

Cataloging

Shared cataloging has been the most successful library automation effort, thanks to the early efforts of bibliographic utilities such as OCLC,

RLIN, UTLAS, and WLN. Microcomputers have found a place in the cataloging area also.

Informatic's MiniMarc System runs on a Computer Automation LSI 220 16-bit microcomputer.[2] The MARC database is received on 500 floppy discs. As records are called up and modified, they are transferred to the library's database. The program has been used extensively for conversion projects.

The National Library of Mexico has proposed an ambitious shared cataloging project to run on Ohio Scientific C3-B microcomputers. It is meant to use Ohio Scientific intelligent terminals and clusters of C3-Bs to handle authority files, a bibliographic file and a holdings file. The system will support interactive cataloging. Participants in the project are reported to be the Organization of American States, the National Council for Science and Technology, and the National University of Mexico.

Southern Illinois University has been a real hotbed of microcomputer activity. Using an Apple II+, programmers there have written a program to index a collection of 78rpm records—an interesting marriage of technologies! The microcomputer was purchased through SIU's Friends of the Library. A sorting program called "Data Cope" has been used successfully to sort the data on floppy discs into the desired order. The system is being expanded to incorporate a 10-megabyte Corvus disc.

The School of Library and Information Science at the University of Missouri, Columbia, has written programs in Level II Basic for the TRS-80 to track the progress of titles through the technical processing units of a local public library.

Card Production

Card production is not a complex operation once the data have been collected. Libraries have used machine-produced cards for a number of years, beginning with early MTST applications using IBM Selectric typewriters, and continuing with the card-production services of national bibliographic centers. Several microcomputer systems have emerged for this application.

Warner-Eddison Associates of Cambridge, Massachusetts, has developed a system which runs on a DEC microcomputer, the PDT 150, and is called Inmagic. The microcomputer has 56k of main memory and can use a variety of peripheral storage devices. The software, primarily a database management system for MARC records, is written in Fortran IV. In addition to providing online access and retrieval with Boolean searching, Inmagic produces catalog cards, spine labels, cards, pockets, accession lists, subject bibliographies, and management reports. Cost of a microcomputer-based turnkey system starts at about $1800. A 5000-record system sells for about $7200 and runs on a small minicomputer.

Information Technologists, a consulting firm specializing in microcomputer-based library automation in the Washington, D.C., area has demonstrated catalog card production using standard "off-the-shelf" software modules. Using a North Star Horizon microcomputer they produced a book catalog for a private law library.

The Brighton Postgraduate Medical Center in Great Britain uses a microcomputer-based word processer, the BDP 90-02, to produce catalog cards for a cataloging cooperative of twelve libraries in the South East Thames Regional Health Authority.[3]

Data Entry

Data-entry applications for microcomputers have been popular because of portability of the hardware and freedom from the scheduling conflicts that often typify time-shared data collection systems. Collection of the data is simpler than managing and retrieving the data; hence many have opted for using microcomputer-based systems for data collection and then passing the data to a larger machine environment for manipulation, storage and retrieval.

Information Access Corporation has been using Apple II microcomputers for database input for their Business Index and Legal Resource Index files. Brodart purchased a number of SOL microcomputers for COM catalog shelflist conversion projects. One notable project was for the Los Angeles County Public Library. Although the SOLs are no longer manufactured, Brodart has made them available to replace the OCR update procedures that are now used by many of Brodart's COM catalog customers.

The University of California at Davis is using a DEC LSI 11/2 to build a cataloging database. The system uses a vendor-developed text-editing package and a locally developed key-entry package. It uses DEC's RT/11 operating system and is written in Fortran and Macro Assembler.

The University of Illinois Library is using a Four Phase microcomputer programmed in Vision for general data entry. This system uses 2.5 megabytes of fixed-disc storage and a comparable amount of removable disc storage.

The School of Library and Information Science at the University of Missouri, Columbia, uses a DEC LSI 11/23 to build an in-house automated reference database with three input terminals and dual floppy discs. The sytem runs on software purchased from Charles River Data Systems. Although the main database now resides on an Amdahl mainframe, the library school hopes to transfer the entire operation to the LSI microcomputer.

The University of Nebraska is using a Mohawk Data System, Series 21 for data entry to a batch acquisition system. The computer has 48k of core memory and uses two eight-inch floppy diskettes with 500k of storage. The CPU for the system is a Z80-based Intel microcomputer and uses Mohawk's Formatted Data Entry Package.

The University of Tennessee is using an IBM 5280 to collect data for its library database, which resides on the university's DEC 10 system. The 5280 provides prompts by field for data entry, and uses floppy-disc mass storage. It has a communications interface to transmit the recorded data and can support multiple terminals.

Serials

Serials control represents the most complex automation challenge in the technical processing area. Even though few really good systems have been written, even on larger machines, microcomputers have begun to have an impact.

Gerald Lundeen, from the Graduate School of Library Studies at the University of Hawaii, reports that he has written a program to generate routing slips for journals received at the GSLS Library on a TRS-80-I. The Integrated Library System at the National Library of Medicine (described earlier) has a journal control subsystem. The master bibliographic file is MARC-compatible, according to NLM, and includes online check-in and routing-slip generation. The system does not yet offer binding control.

Public Services

The public services area was one of the first areas of the library to feel the impact of automation, notably in early circulation system projects. It is in the public sector that microcomputers are likely to have their biggest impact, especially in the home-library interface and in the development of "user-friendly" interfaces to complex databases.

Circulation

The ILS system at NLM includes a circulation subsystem. Its developers emphasize that it is a "collection control" system, not just a circulation control system. In more general terms, it is an "inventory" system, not an "absence" system. It has all the standard features of systems running on larger machines, including bar-code labels and light pens. A unique feature of the sytem is the ability to check items temporarily into a named *cart* and later discharge them onto the shelf (when the cart has been emptied) with a single wand stroke. It attempts to specify the exact whereabouts of all books at all times. Planned expansion of the system will include online catalog access and a portable data-entry system for "shelf-reading" inventory.

The Standard Telecommunications Laboratory in Great Britain has a circulation system for a slide collection which runs on an Exidy Sorcerer.[4] The microcomputer has 32k of main memory and uses two 125k discs. The system, written in-house by a librarian, manages the 10,000-item slide collection. It is an absence system, and data are keyed in at the point of transaction.

The Oak Ridge (Oregon) Public Library has a similar system running on an Ohio Scientific C2-8 PDF. It uses a database management package purchased from Ohio Scientific to manage an annual circulation of 17,000. The librarian, who is the only staff member, was being "drowned" in paperwork, and is now free to manage the collection and handle reference questions.

A number of circulation systems running on larger machines use microcomputers in support roles. Typical of these is the system at Oberlin College. The main system, written originally for Bucknell University, runs on the campus Sigma 9 mainframe. The Intel 8080 microcomputer serves as a front end for the system, and acts as a backup when the Sigma is down. The Intel handles the user interface, formats the transactions for the Sigma, and handles traffic control between seven terminals and the mainframe. The microcomputer uses 48k of main memory and is presently using floppy-disc storage. There are plans to expand the system to Winchester-type hard discs in the future.

There are a number of backups for the Computer Library Services, Inc. (CLSI) circulation system that have been written on Apple II+ microcomputers. Two examples of these are those in use at Johns Hopkins University and at the University of California, Santa Barbara. The Johns Hopkins system uses a Winchester-type hard disc and a Sony Triniton terminal. The Santa Barbara system was developed by Computer Translator, Inc., Provo, Utah, and uses Apple-Soft, Integer Basic, and a Paper Tiger printer. In addition, they are using a word-processing package from Apple for other library applications.

Cincinnati Electronics reportedly has a scaled-down version of their Classic system which runs on a microcomputer as an absence-based circulation system.[5]

Media Centers

An early application of microcomputers in media centers was the Children's Media Database developed by Ted Hines on an Apple II+ at the University of North Carolina, Greensboro.

A commercial turnkey system for media centers has been developed by Research Technology, Inc. The film-booking system, called AMMS (Automated Media Management System), runs on a General Automation 220. It boasts 64k of main memory and 10 megabytes of disc storage. With a single video terminal and a printer, the system and software sell for just under $50,000. The software is written in Pascal, and the system can be expanded to four terminals.

The Health Science Library at St. Luke's Methodist Hospital in Cedar Rapids, Iowa, has been doing development work on an Apple II+. In addition to an audiovisual inventory system, staff are using the Apple to generate book orders and keep interlibrary loan statistics, and they are developing CAI programs for user orientation and continuing education activities at the hospital.

The School of Library and Information Science at Indiana University has developed a media equipment control system on a Vector Graphics microcomputer. Additional research investigating possible uses of the microcomputer in small Indiana libraries is currently underway.

Reference

UCLA has been experimenting with its REFLES system—Reference Librarian Enhancement System. Designed to run on several different microcomputers, it contains a database of search strategies and ephemeral data. Richard Marcus at the Massachusetts Institute of Technology reportedly has been investigating the possible uses of the microcomputer in reference services.

Current Awareness

The Cincinnati Country Day School Library has been creating subject bibliographies using a program developed in-house on an Apple II+. Work there is progressing on an acquisition system, which will also run on the Apple.

Interlibrary Loan

The University of Missouri, Columbia, has developed a program on a TRS-80 which the local public library uses as a Telenet host. The program enables the library to communicate with other libraries within the local and state library networks regarding interlibrary loan requests and general electronic mail messages.

Database Front-End Processer

Database searching has been an area primarily dominated by professionals because of the complexity of retrieval. The variety of command languages from one system to another has made searching by the end user very difficult. Several alternatives using microcomputers have recently been developed.

Ol'Sam (On-line Database Search Assistance Machine) has been developed by the Franklin Institute Research Laboratories. It runs on a North

Star Horizon microcomputer or other Pascal microsystems. The North Star configuration uses 64k of main memory with 36k of floppy-diskette secondary storage. The system can multiplex the work of two searchers through a single telephone line. It uses a common query language for DIALOG, SDC and NLM. It includes CAI programs that teach online searching offline to save line charges. The system maintains an administrative log of all search activity, and monitors strategy patterns in order to suggest more productive strategies.

The Computer Corporation of America has announced the availability of its Chemical Automated Search Terminal (CAST) System, which is designed especially for chemical information centers. It consists of a CCA microcomputer with 64k of main memory and dual floppy-disc drives. It includes a 1200 baud modem and a printer. The system can access MED-LARS, ICC Chemical Information System, DIALOG, ORBIT, and customized databases.

One of the most interesting microcomputer-based front-end processers was developed at Dartmouth College in conjunction with an online catalog pilot project. The microcomputer used was a Terak 8510A with 24k of main memory and floppy-disc secondary storage. The system, written in Pascal, accesses a Bibliographic Retrieval Services (BRS) database of MARC records built from Dartmouth's OCLC tapes. The MARC records were mapped into standard BRS paragraphs. The Terak prompts the user responses and translates them into BRS commands. The retrieved records can be scanned, stored and manipulated.

Storage and Retrieval

Storage and retrieval systems differ from front-end processers in that they store and manage the information as well as retrieve it. These systems on microcomputers are limited by the storage capacity of microcomputer peripherals, but can still handle quite a respectable database.

Cuadra Associates has developed a system called STAR. It runs on an Alpha Micro, a 16-bit microcomputer with 128k of main memory, and secondary storage of 90 megabytes. Along with a video terminal and printer, the system sells for approximately $40,000. The system allows one to build a customized database. Retrieval by Boolean searching is available. A photocomposition interface allows the user to produce finished copy without an intermediate typesetting step. The system is expandable to eight linked microcomputers which can support a total of 2400 megabytes of disc storage, or close to 4.8 million MARC records.

On the other end of the scale, the California Library Authority for Systems and Services (CLASS) is making available a turnkey retrieval system using a TRS-80 II for about $5000.[6] The system is based on the Golden Retriever developed at Golden Gate University. A new version, which will run on an Apple computer, reportedly is called Golden Delicious. The system is said to have great potential for circulation or management of small databases.

The Institute for Scientific Information's PRIMATE system also features a database management system which may be used for filing journal articles, memos, correspondence, documents, etc. It can store up to 10,000 records which can be retrieved by keyword. The system can also be used as a front-end processer for online systems such as SDC, BRS and Euronet.

Reserve Book Room

Southern Illinois University has used Apple II+ microcomputers to great advantage in the library's Reserve Book Room. Using Apple-Writer, which they purchased for $75, the staff sends form letters to the faculty requesting and confirming reserve lists. They also use the program to produce bibliographies and search guides for the Library Instruction Office. As items are recalled or requested, they are noted in the system. The output serves as a "high activity" book report, from which the subject librarian considers items in the collection for duplication. Currently being developed is a music reserve catalog, which will include a shelf list, a composer/title index and a course/instructor index.

General Use

Susan Hussie, from the Gretna (Nebraska) Public Library, reports that she uses her microcomputer to schedule activities held at the library. It keeps track of hours worked, vacation and sick leave for all employees. It prepares the budget, conducts the inventory, and prepares book orders. It handles interlibrary loan records, generates lists of fines for collection by the sheriff, and in its spare time, waters the grass and regulates the heat.[7]

Management

Although library management seems a natural for automation efforts, this area has not been influenced heavily by automated systems. Although management modules have been added to circulation and acquisition systems, among others, few stand-alone management systems have been written. Microcomputers are, however, finding their way into library front offices.

Word Processing

Word processing is occurring in libraries in all sizes of machines. A few examples of microcomputer applications are mentioned here.

California Stae University at Northridge is using an Apple II+ for word processing. The "write-on" software module from Apple has been used successfully to prepare personnel budget projections. Visicalc has also been used for general ledger work in the fiscal office. The system uses a Hy-Type I printer.

Iowa State University is using a Xerox 800 with the vendor's word-processing software for general office production.

Ohio State University purchased a CPT 800 for word processing. It uses 64k of main memory, two eight-inch floppy discs and a Rotary V daisywheel printer. In addition to CPT's Word Processing Package, CP/M Basic is available so the machine can be programmed locally. The system has been used for general correspondence, production of exhibit catalogs, statistical reports for the circulation department, and fund reports for the acquisitions department. The system was purchased by the OSU Friends of the Library.

The University of Western Ontario uses a WD78 word processer with 16k of main memory to maintain personnel files, salary data and statistics. Programmed in Basic, Fortran and Dibol, the machine functions as a front end to the university's DEC 10 mainframe computer.

Southern Illinois University uses an IBM Display writer for general word processing.

Mailing Lists

The Standard Telecommunications Laboratory in Great Britain maintains a mailing list and generates mailing labels on an Exidy Sorcerer.[8] The system uses floppy-disc storage and a commercial software package.

Library Statistics

Southern Illinois University uses an Apple II+ and Visicalc to produce comparative and cumulative statistics for the library's circulation department. A monthly traffic count is maintained, as are the Higher Education General Information Survey (HEGIS) reference statistics. The staff reports that what was formerly a three-day project each month is now performed in forty minutes. Additionally, they are able to generate data that were impractical to collect manually.

Personnel

Southern Illinois University Library is also maintaining a personnel list on its Apple II+. From it are generated internal telephone directories, mailing lists, and a library committee list which includes dates and terms of office. Plans are underway to expand the use of the machine to maintain a number of indexes for library materials. The work is being done with a purchased database management software package.

Friends of the Library

The Saint Louis County Public Library maintains an address list of book donors on its microcomputer. The staff sends acknowledgment letters and meeting announcements to those on the file. A list of library periodical subscriptions is also being maintained.[9]

Other Applications

Research

The microcomputer is a good tool for research, since it can be set up for a project without the extensive and expensive site preparation that larger machines require. The cost of the microcomputer can be included in the grant proposal, and in fact, research on microcomputers is quite attractive to many granting foundations.

Clarion State College in Pennsylvania has set up a microcomputer laboratory with Radio Shack TRS-80s to develop circulation, reference files and union lists for small- and medium-sized rural libraries.[10]

Library schools in Great Britain are doing a great deal of research with microcomputers in the areas of teaching library skills and user interfaces. For example, the College of Librarianship, Wales, is using a Hewlett-Packard 2645A and a microcomputer with floppy discs to teach subject indexing and to construct subject indexes.[11]

The University of Manchester has received a British Libary grant to research the use of microcomputers to simplify the searching of online systems. The work, which is being done in the Computation Department of the Institute of Science and Technology, consists of an automatic translation between the command languages for Euronet, DIALOG and SDC. The interface includes simplified user dialogs, help modules and tutorials. Dr. P.W. Williams is the principal investigator.[12]

At Aston University, a project team headed by Steven Jamieson is using a specially developed microcomputer to develop and test sophisticated retrieval techniques, incluidng relevance-weighting of terms. When perfected on the microcomputer, the techniques will be used at City University, London, to search MEDLINE on BLAISE.[13]

The Central Information Service (CIS) at the University College, London, has done extensive work on microcomputers.[14] Researchers there have simulated DIALOG on a Commodore Pet to teach online searching inexpensively. The program includes a computer-assisted instruction course on search strategy. The software is available from the school on a cassette.[15] A similar program is being written for the Apple. Other applications at CIS are a survey analysis program similar to SPSS, and a mailing list program. "Word Craft," a package developed by Dataview Microcomputer Systems, is being used for word processing. CIS has also written simulation programs to teach the creation of accession lists, a MARC editor, and a simulated circulation system.

The University of Sheffield and the University of Pittsburgh are also reported to be using a DIALOG simulation on a Commodore Pet.

OCLC's Channel 2000 project, with the Home Delivery of Library Information program, used a Motorola 6800 microcomputer. The system used a standard telephone set for communication, a standard television set as a monitor, and a keypad for data input. The 6800 can display graphics as well as text. Automatic log-on and log-off capability was built into the microcomputers. The system provided access to mainframe files that included an encyclopedia, library service news, catalog access, community information, and financial services.

Electronic Mail

Edunet, a subsidiary of Educom, has announced the availability of its EASY network access system. Developed at the University of Wisconsin, the system uses an Apple II+ microcomputer. The Apple acts as an interactive terminal to upload files from diskette to Edumail and download messages to its diskette to be examined offline. Connect time on Telenet is reduced drastically, thereby cutting the costs of electronic mail on the system.[16]

Microcomputers as Media

Perhaps the most visible front-office use of microcomputers in libraries is the use of microcomputers as media. The Palo Alto (California) Public Library purchased several microcomputers through its Friends of the Library group for use in the Children's Room. The library stacks programs on cassettes for use in the machines, and has reported heavy and enthusiastic use. The library also is participating in a computer literacy project in the community.[17]

Ohio State University has installed coin-operated Ataris in its Browsing Room and West Campus Learning Resources Center. Each location has an Atari 800, a color monitor, a cassette deck, and prerecorded software. The vendor supplying the microcomputers, Computer Bus, collects the first $25 of income per machine each week, and the library receives the balance. The vendor supplies $150 of software for each machine, and has Commodore Pet microcomputers available, as well as the 400 and 800 Atari models. The user pays twenty-five cents for a 15-minue block of time.

Other libraries providing microcomputers for public use include the Chicago Public Library (Commodore Pet), State of Minnesota Department of Education (200 Apple II+s), the Portage, Michigan, school system (20 Commodore Pets), Menlo Park (California) Public Library (TRS-80s,

Ataris and Commodore Pets), Plattsburgh (New York) Public Library (Apples), Columbus (Ohio) Public Library (9 microcomputers in the main library and 7 in branch libraries).[18]

Microcomputers in School Media Centers

The Pennsylvania Department of Education has encouraged the purchase and use of microcomputers in school media centers. It sponsors an annual Management Awareness Day focusing on microcomputers, and publishes *A Guide to Microcomputers*[19] and *A Guide to Microcomputer Software*[20] for teachers and administrators within the system.

The American Association of School Librarians sponsored a technical session at the 1981 ALA Midwinter meeting in Washington, D.C., on new technology in school media centers. Microcomputers were at the forefront of the discussion. Follow-up meetings are planned for subsequent ALA meetings.

Future Developments

In the area of hardware technology we can expect better and less expensive peripherals. The cost of peripherals can now easily exceed the price of the microcomputer. Fast, inexpensive dot matrix printers will replace the slower, expensive impact printers now typical in a microcomputer configuration. Bubble memory and videodisc technology will push back the storage barriers. The development of larger and faster core memory will speed the processing capability of the microcomputers themselves. Better and more strongly supported languages and operating systems will emerge, such as "Unix," "C," "Ada," and "Forth."

The most important breakthroughs will be in the area of reliable networking. Already, public libraries such as the Pikes Peak Library in Colorado Springs have many users accessing the library system on their own home microcomputers. As network protocols are worked out, we will have access to a truly national resource on our own personal computers in the comfort and privacy of our living rooms.

REFERENCES

1. Winfield, R.P. "An Informal Survey of Operational Microprocesser-based Systems." *Program: Automated Library and Information Systems* 14(July 1980):126.
2. Simpson, George A. *Microcomputers in Library Automation.* McLean, Va.: MITRE Corp., 1978, p. 20.
3. Winfield, "Informal Survey," p. 126.
4. Ibid., pp. 121-26.
5. Simpson, *Microcomputers*, p. 17.

6. *Advanced Technology Libraries* 9(July 1980):7.

7. Kloepper, Dan. "Maxi-Mini-Micro: Microcomputers in Libraries, 15 November 1982." *Nebraska Library Association Quarterly* 8(Winter 1977):30-32.

8. Winfield, "Informal Survey."

9. *Information Retrieval and Library Automation* 16(1980):4.

10. "Computers for Rural Libraries." *LJ/SLJ Hotline* 10(2 March 1981):4.

11. "Using Terminals with Text Editor Facilities for Teaching Index Construction." *British Library Research and Development Newsletter* 20(May 1980):6.

12. "Enhancement of On-line Information Retrieval Using a Microprocesser-Assisted Terminal." *British Library Research and Development Newsletter* 20(May 1980):2.

13. "Interactive Information Retrieval Through an Intelligent Terminal." *British Library Research and Development Newsletter* 20(May 1980):1.

14. Vickery A., and Brooks, H. "Microcomputer, Liberator or Enslaver." In *Fourth International Online Information Meeting, London, 9-11 December 1980*, pp. 387-96. Oxford, Eng.: Learned Information, 1980.

15. "CIS Software Series." *FID News Bulletin* 30(July/Aug. 1980):60.

16. "EASY Cuts EDUMAIL Costs." *Edunet News* 23(Spring 1981):6.

17. "Personal Computer in the Children's Room." *LJ/SLJ Hotline* 10(2 March 1981):4.

18. Lundeen, Gerald. "The Role of Microcomputers in Libraries." *Wilson Library Bulletin* 55(Nov. 1980):178-85.

19. Douglas, Shirley, and Neights, Gary. *A Guide to Microcomputers.* Nazareth, Pa.: Colonial Northampton Intermediate Unit, 1980.

20. _____ . *A Guide to Instructional Microcomputer Software.* Nazareth, Pa.: Colonial Northampton Intermediate Unit, 1980.

DAVID R. HOYT
Technical Information Specialist
U.S. Department of Agriculture

Word Processer Applications at the USDA's Technical Information Systems

Introduction

Since this is a clinic on library applications of data processing, we ought to be able to answer a few very basic questions before proceeding with the topic of word processer applications at the U.S. Department of Agriculture. First, why do we want to automate our libraries and their numerous operations? Is it self-evidently necessary that we do so? Is automation in all its many, varied forms, in and of itself, always a good thing? When is it not? Second, given the widespread availability of inexpensive and easy-to-use hardware and flexible software, what, within our libraries, do we want to bring under automation's electronic control? Should our long-range goal be to automate everything from the reference interview (now possible with voice-activated and voice-responding machines) to the traditional functions of cataloging and indexing? What about management? Can the management of a large library be automated? In short, is our goal to automate everything the librarian now does? And if not everything, then what should not be automated? And what is the principle by which we determine what can and cannot be accomplished automatically? I suggest that we must be able to answer these questions before we can proceed with an intelligent discussion of our topic.

All of these questions, in fact, can be answered, and the answers are surprisingly simple. The basis of our argument is this: anything which can be specified can be automated. Anything which we cannot specify we cannot automate. All those activities of the first category belong to the province of the machine. They should be automated. Human intelligence,

This paper is exempt from U.S. copyright.

imagination and creativity are too precious to expend energy on them. On the other hand, all of the items of the second category—the ambiguous, the indeterminate, the complex—belong to the province of the librarian. The librarian's sole task, therefore, is to separate the two orders, to bring under the control of the machine the first category (the specifiable), and to bring under the control of the mind the second category (the ambiguous, the amorphous, the complex). The true task of the librarian, then, is managing complexity.

With this as a preface, let me proceed directly with my topic—the application of word processers at the U.S. Department of Agriculture's Technical Information Systems (TIS). I want to share some of the many activities, reports and processes which we have found necessary to automate via word processors. In using the term *word processers*, I am referring primarily to the Lanier No Problem word processer. It is the one machine which we have found most suitable for our needs. There are many different kinds of word processers, and you should probably check with a representative of each to determine which will suit your specific needs. Also, note that I make no distinction between the Lanier word processer and a computer. As far as I am concerned, the differences are only those of degree, not of kind. The Lanier is a fully programmable, stand-alone device. It is capable of adding, subtracting, calculating, accepting alpha or numeric data, storing, sorting, searching, matching and displaying these data. We have even programmed our Laniers to communicate with outside, off-site, mainframe information retrieval systems, such as Lockheed's DIALOG and BRS. We regard the Lanier, therefore, as a fully operational computing system. We have dozens of different applications for our word processers. Because our applications are diverse, I have grouped them according to three classifications: (1) management information systems, (2) program support systems, and (3) online information retrieval systems.

Management Information Systems

Technical Information Systems is a large and complex organization, with a staff of 264 people, a budget of over $9 million, a 15-story library building in Beltsville, Maryland, and a collection of over 1.7 million items. We produce our own databases, offer current-awareness literature services and online information retrieval services, and operate a regional document delivery system which spans the entire continent. To provide these services, we must employ a staff which includes not only catalogers, indexers and reference librarians, but computer programmers, systems analysts and administrative personnel as well. The support personnel include mailroom clerks, building engineers, heating and air conditioning specialists, and more. Managing such an organization is complex. To enable the administrator to manage this complexity, we have endeavored to automate all of the routine functions which we could identify and describe. In the realm of management information, most of this has been accomplished on the Lanier.

Consider first the organization chart (fig. 1). An administration needs to know where people in an organization are at all times for the most efficient grouping of their talents. The Repagination program allows us to create charts, draw blocks and diagrams, and move them around at will to maintain an accurate and up-to-date picture of the way the agency's personnel resources are organized. It also enables us to visualize alternative structures, an important theoretical activity.

Second, we automated the agency's phone directory. At last, we have an up-to-date phone book, another simple and routine function suitable for the word processor.

Next on the list of management information systems is our Personnel Breakdown program (see fig. 2). Here the picture begins to get complicated. This chart shows the various categories of employment, and the relative strengths of the individual units within Technical Information Systems. As a government agency, we have numerous categories of employment ranging from permanent full-time to temporary part-time. Keeping track of our employment picture can be complicated. Again, this is a management information system designed to give the administrator feedback about his personnel resources.

At any given point in time, we may have dozens of outstanding personnel actions: promotions, resignations, transfers to other units, changes in status, etc. In 1980 alone we processed over 500 separate personnel actions. We now keep track of these on a word processor, which can alert us if an action has been outstanding for an unacceptable length of time (see fig. 3). By updating this information regularly, the administrator can spot actions moving too slowly through the system and take action before a crisis develops. Again, this is an important management tool for keeping in touch with the flux of reality.

Our Personnel Funds Report is an application for which the word processor was especially designed. The Personnel Funds Report is used to keep track of the payroll (no small task when it is over $3 million). It is a complicated but routine report cosisting of employees' names, positions, pay scales, salary types, hours worked, hours cumulated, salaries earned, and other bits of essential information. Compiling this report manually for 264 people used to be an immense task. Using the Math Master/Snap program designed by Lanier, it is now nearly automatic. Once the necessary elements and data have been identified, the machine calculates the rest of the information and produces a report. What is remarkable about this process is that the word processor is performing as a fully functional

OFFICE OF THE ADMINISTRATOR
AND
OFFICE OF ASSOCIATE ADMINISTRATOR

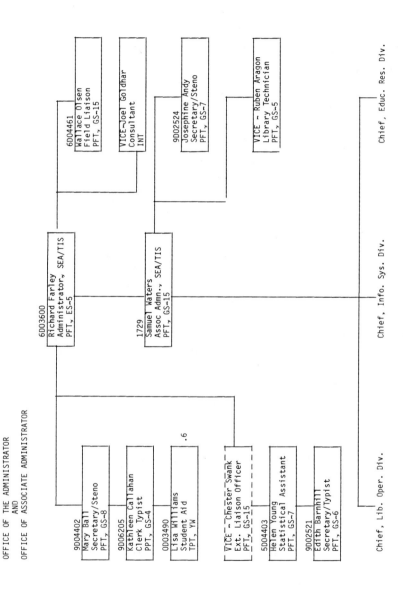

6D03600
Richard Farley
Administrator, SEA/TIS
PFT, ES-5

6D04461
Wallace Olsen
Field Liaison
PFT, GS-15

VICE-Joel Goldhar
Consultant
INT

1729
Samuel Waters
Assoc Admn., SEA/TIS
PFT, GS-15

9D02524
Josephine Andy
Secretary/Steno
PFT, GS-7

VICE - Ruben Aragon
Library Technician
PFT, GS-5

9D04402
Mary Ball
Secretary/Steno
PFT, GS-8

9D06205
Kathleen Callahan
Clerk Typist
PPT, GS-4

0D03490
Lisa Williams
Student Aid
TPT, YW

.6

VICE - Chester Swank
Ext. Liaison Officer
PFT, GS-15

5D04403
Helen Young
Statistical Assistant
PFT, GS-7

9D02521
Edith Barnhill
Secretary/Typist
PFT, GS-6

Chief, Lib. Oper. Div.

Chief, Info. Sys. Div.

Chief, Educ. Res. Div.

Fig. 1. Organization Chart for the USDA Technical Information Systems Office

Unit	PFT on duty	PFT vac	PPT on duty	PPT vac	FTT/TPT on duty	FTT/TPT vac	Student Aids YWs on duty	YWs vac	GWs on duty	GWs vac	VACANT TOTAL	ON DUTY TOTAL	GRAND TOTAL
OFF. OF ADMN.	07	02*	01	00	00	01	01	00	00	00	03	09	12
SUB-TOTAL	07	02	01	00	00	01	01	00	00	00	03	09	12
LIB. OPER. DIV.	02	01	00	00	01	00	00	00	00	00	01	03	04
ACQUISITIONS BR	02	00	00	00	04***	00	00	00	00	00	00	06	06
SER CTRL & EXCH	18	01	02	03	00	00	01	00	00	00	04	21	25
SEL. & ORD. SECT.	10	00	00	00	03	01	01	00	00	00	01	14	15
ANALYSIS BRANCH	01	00	00	00	00	01	00	00	00	00	01	01	02
CATALOGING SECT.	18	03**	00	04	00	00	00	00	01	01	08	19	27
INDEXING SECT.	15	01	00	04	00	00	00	01	00	00	06	15	21
LEND/REF BRANCH	00	00	00	00	00	00	00	00	00	00	00	00	00
LENDING SECTION	01	01	00	00	00	00	00	00	00	00	01	01	02
UTILIZ. UNIT	19	03	00	00	00	00	00	00	06	02*	05	25	30
MAINT. UNIT	13	02	00	00	01	00	00	00	04	00	02	18	20
REFERENCE SECT.	01	01	00	00	00	00	00	00	00	00	01	01	02
AUT. RET. UNIT	04	00	00	00	00	00	00	00	01	00	00	05	05
INFO & BIB UNIT	07	01	00	00	00	00	00	00	01	00	01	08	09
FLD & DEPART BR.	00	01*	00	00	00	00	00	01	00	00	02	00	02
DC BRANCH	06	00	02	01	00	00	00	00	02	00	01	10	11
LAW BRANCH	04	00	01	01	00	00	00	00	00	00	01	05	06
SUB-TOTAL	121	15	05	13	09	02	02	02	15	03	35	152	187
INFO SYS DIV.	03	00	00	00	00	00	00	00	00	00	00	03	03
SYSTEMS DEV. BR.	04	00	00	00	02****	00	00	00	00	00	00	06	06
SYS ADMN & MGNT BR	11	00	01	00	00	00	00	00	00	00	00	12	12
LIB SYS BRANCH	12	00	01	00	01	00	00	00	04	01	01	18	19
TECH PROD SER BR.	04	00	00	00	00	00	00	00	00	00	00	04	04
SUB-TOTAL	34	00	02	00	03	00	00	00	04	01	01	43	44
EDUC RES DIVISION	10	00	00	00	00	00	00	00	00	00	00	10	10
FOOD NUTR INFO CT	06	00	01	00	00	03	00	00	01	00	03	08	11
SUB-TOTAL	16	00	01	00	00	03	00	00	01	00	03	18	21
TOTALS:	178	17	09	13	12	06	03	02	20	04	42	222	264

	TIS CEIL.	ON DUTY	APRD NO 52's VAC / CUM VAC	TOTAL
PFT	188	178	17	195
AO	31	21	19	40
SA	25	23	06	29
IPA'S	02	01	01	02
	246	223	43	266

*- includes 1 NOT FUNDED position.
**- includes 2 NOT FUNDED positions.
***- includes 3 Coop. Educ. Stu. – New Mex. Highlands Univ. on LWOP until June,1981.
****- includes 1 Coop. Educ. Stu. – Univ. Maryland on LWOP.

Fig. 2. Personnel Breakdown of TIS Units—FY1981

CNTR #	DIV-UNIT	ACTION	NAME	CURRENT POSITION	APPROVED BY RAF	PROPOSED EFF. DATE	STATUS & DATE	COMPLETED DATE
TIS-493	0-OA	Recruit	Vice-Soden, J.	Stud Aid/YV	08/20/80			
TIS-494	L-LAW	Recruit	Vice-Hamilton,Y.	Lib Stu Aid/GW-1	08/20/80			
TIS-495	L-SC&E	Resign-Summer	Vice-Lee, A.	Clk Typ/GS-2	08/20/80	08/22/80		
TIS-496	L-UTL	Termination	MackLin, Sharon	Lib Aid/GW-3	08/20/80	08/22/80		
TIS-497	L-CAT	Prom/GS-4	Millard, Irene	Clk Typ/GS-3	08/22/80	08/24/80		
TIS-498	I-LSB	Pay Adj PT	Jefferys, Maria	Stu Aid/GW-2	08/22/80	08/26/80		
TIS-499	I-LSB	Pay Adj PT	Clark, Mary	Comp Aid/GW-3	08/22/80	08/25/80		
TIS-500	L-MNT	LWOP-11/30/80	Ho, Judy	Lib Tech/GS-6	08/22/80	08/24/80		
TIS-501	L-UTL	Pay Adj PT	Butler, James	Lib Stu Aid/GW-2	08/22/80	08/24/80		
TIS-502	L-UTL	Ext Temp Appt	Butler, James	Lib Stu Aid/GW-2	08/22/80	09/27/80		
TIS-503	L-CAT	Prom/GS-5	Souder, Shirley	Lib Tech/GS-4	08/22/80	09/21/80		
TIS-504	L-SC&E	Resign	Morris, Bernadine	Lib Stu Aid/GW-1	08/22/80	08/29/80		
TIS-505	L-SC&E	Recruit	Vice-Morris, B.	Lib Stu Aid/GW-1	08/22/80	ASAP		
TIS-506	L-MNT	Pay Adj PT	Vaughn, Daryle	Lib Stu Aid/GW-2	08/22/80	08/18/80		
TIS-507	L-MNT	Pay Adj PT	Barton, Judine	Lib Stu Aid/GW-2	08/22/80	08/18/80		
TIS-508	L-I&B	Pay Adj PT	McKellar, Karen	Lib Stu Aid/GW-1	08/26/80	08/24/80		
TIS-509	L-SEL	Termination	Humphrey, Curtis	Summer Aid/YW	08/26/80	08/29/80		
TIS-510	L-UTL	Termination	Simms, Johnetta	Lib Stu Aid/GW-1	08/26/80	08/15/80		
TIS-511	L-SC&E	Termination	Sevier, Kimberly	Summer Aid/YW	08/27/80	08/29/80		
TIS-512	L-LAW	Prom/Pay Adj	Cureton, Adger	Lib Stu Aid/GW-1	08/28/80	09/07/80		
TIS-513	L-LAW	Resign	Richards, Valarie	Lib Stu Aid/GW-2	08/28/80	08/29/80	Cancel	
TIS-514	L-I&B	Chg Duty Hrs	Brown, Jesse	Lib Tech/GS-5	08/28/80	09/01/80		
TIS-515	I-MIS	Resign	Gallagher, Wendy	Sect Typ/GS-5	08/28/80	09/20/80		
TIS-516	L-UTL	Chg Duty Hrs	Raff, Nancy	Lib Tech/GS-5	08/29/80	08/24/80		
TIS-517	L-UTL	Pay Adj PT	Hall, Gayle	Lib Stu Aid/GW-2	08/29/80	09/07/80		
TIS-518	L-UTL	Pay Adj PT	Little, Angela	Lib Stu Aid/GW-1	08/29/80	08/17/80		
TIS-519	I-ISD	Appoint	Paulsen, Gerald	Comp Sys Ayt/GS-13	09/02/80	09/07/80		
TIS-520	I-ISD	Reassign	Warnick, Edward	Comp Prog/GS-11	09/02/80	Immed		
TIS-521	L-UTL	Pay Adj PT	Raff, Nancy	Lib Tech/GS-5	09/03/80	09/07/80		
TIS-522	L-SC&E	Pay Adj PT	Black, Dreama	Lib Tech/GS-5	09/03/80	09/07/80		
TIS-523	OD-LAW	Retire	Jones, Robert	LEG Spec/GS-11	09/04/80	08/29/80		
TIS-524	I-ISD	Recruit	Vice Sue Biederman	Comp Tech/GS-4	09/04/80	ASAP		
TIS-525	I-LOD	Termination	Pratt, Sheri	Clk Typ/GS-2	09/05/80	08/23/80		
TIS-526	I-ISD	Play Adj PT	Swan, Charles	Comp Tech/GW-2	09/09/80	09/02/80		
TIS-527	I-FNIC	Temorary	Chisholm, Thomas	Lib Stu Aid/GW-3	09/09/80	10/01/80		
TIS-528	L-SC&E	Pay Adj PT	Reeves, Gerald	Lib Tech/GW-5	09/12/80			
TIS-529	I-ISD	Reassign	Lin, T.	Comp Prog/GS-9	09/12/80			
TIS-530	I-ISD	Reassign	Spahn, Carl	Comp Tech/GS-5	09/12/80			
TIS-531	L-DCB	Promotion	Cheney, Sheldon	Librn	09/12/80			

Fig. 3. SF-52 Personnel Actions—FY1980
(TIS Personnel Funds Report)

automatic computer—adding, subtracting, calculating, updating and modifying data, and producing a fresh report every other week. For this application, we use the Records Manager and Math Master programs. By using these programs, we maintain better control over the flow of funds.

The next application is very interesting, but simple. Suppose you want to know who in the organization speaks Basque, or possesses a special skill, or who was assigned to be a representative to a special analysis budget team for nutrition standards or some other topic. For an organization as large as ours, assignments such as these and identification of special skills can be immensely difficult. To solve this problem and provide management with essential information about who is doing what, or going where, we developed the Official Representation Special Assignments, and Areas of Specialization database. We create and update this database on the Lanier, and circulate it frequently among the staff for improved communications and better coordination. It is amazing how people come forth with their own skills once they see what somebody else has identified on this list as their own.

An accompaniment to this is the SEA/TIS Travel and Meeting Calendar. This calendar lists scheduled meetings outside the agency, and allows us to keep track of who is going where, when, and for what. This is an essential tool for coordinating outside activities and maximizing the use of scarce travel resources. No longer can the left hand be accused of not knowing what the right hand is doing. For this application, we use the Repagination program.

The next two items are crucial to the successful management of every large organization, and their importance cannot be overemphasized. They are the Operating Plan and the Status of Funds Report. The operating plan is a statement, by individual units and divisions, of how much money is available to spend in a given fiscal year, how it is expected to be obligated, and what funds have actually been spent thus far (status of funds). The operating plan is the primary tool used by management for controlling the budget, establishing priorities for the disbursement of funds, and maintaining control over the budgetary process. The word processer enables us to maintain an accurate and current picture of our internal state of fiscal affairs. Without it, I cannot imagine how we could manage a $9 million budget. Each secretary for each division keeps the records for that division, and inputs the data into a word processer in the administrator's office. By using fixed formats, standardized terminology (i.e., object class categories) and procedures, we are able to keep firm control of what could easily become chaotic. In short, we are once again managing complexity by automating routine functions using the word processer. The word processer also allows retrieval of selected bits of information, such as how much has been spent on training, or travel, or database management, and produces separate reports on any given aspect of the budget. Managers often want to know how much has already been spent on a particular class of items, but are unable to extract the information because of inflexible budgetary procedures. The word processer's Financial program enabled us to change that situation at TIS.

The larger budgetary process itself is outlined in figure 4, which shows that at any given point in time, we are working on three separate budgets simultaneously: the current year's operating budget, the next fiscal year's budget request working its way through Congress, and the following year's budgetary estimates and justifications being submitted to USDA and the president's Office of Management and Budget. This chart helps us to keep track of the whole process. While the politics of a budget are complex, and could never be automated, the figures and write-ups can—and should be.

Finally, we are constantly called upon to prepare special reports for higher management about our Equal Employment Opportunity and Affirmative Action or other special programs; the word processer produces charts to satisfy these requests. We use the Lanier to calculate our personnel profile, indicate minority hiring, their grades, percentages of the whole staff, promotions, etc. Once the data have been input, the reports can be generated and updated almost automatically. We use the Math Master/ Snap program to generate these reports.

As can be seen from the above examples, our use of the word processer for supporting management's information needs is extensive, and the earlier applications are not even exhaustive. By utilizing the various records management, financial management, math, and other programs, we are able at any given moment to know how our personnel and financial resources are allocated, and to what activity they are committed. This has resulted in a tremendous improvement in the efficiency with which management expends energy, and, correspondingly, it has resulted in an overall improvement of the agency's operating environment. Confusion, chaos and overlap are, if not eliminated, at least greatly reduced.

Program Support Systems

Our use of the word processer for program support is not as extensive as it is for management information systems. The reason for this is probably twofold. First, our major products, such as the AGRICOLA and CRIS (Current Research Information System) databases, are too large to be either created or managed on word processers, though this may change in the future. For this we depend on outside commercial systems, such as DIA-LOG Information Retrieval Services and the Washington Computer Center. Second, while word processers have been utilized by management for

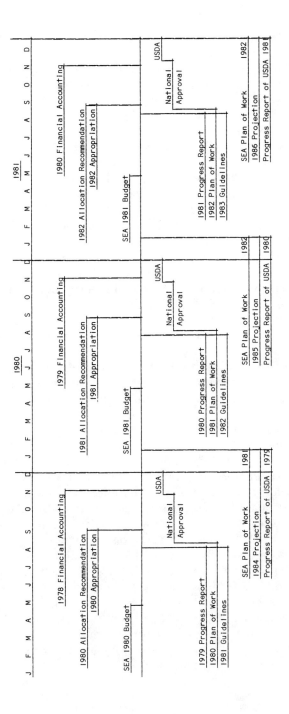

Fig. 4. Calendar Outline of Budgets of Technical Information Systems Office

several years for administrative support, they are just now beginning to be used in program support areas, and we have not fully discovered their potential. We have used them to create and track our "management by objectives" (MBO) reports. (These are clearly worded statements of objectives linked to program activities, which show accomplishments and milestones toward completion. We have tracked our MBOs on word processers for more than five years.) We use the Lanier in program areas primarily for storing and updating essential information necessary to create and search the databases. This includes items such as the AGRICOLA category codes, CRIS classification codes, and Current Awareness Literature Service (CALS) retrieval codes. These are extensive alphanumeric classification schemes used in indexing AGRICOLA, profiling for CALS, and CRIS or AGRICOLA database searching. These classification manuals are lengthy and complicated, and would be difficult to manage, update or prepare for publication on non—word-processing equipment. In the future we expect to discover more innovative uses of the information, since it is now stored in machine-readable form.

Another very important use of the Lanier in a program area relies on its ability to handle mailing labels and correspondence. Using the List Merge program, we can create and store several hundred mailing labels; sort these labels by zip code, last name or other alphabetic descriptor; search the list by state or descriptive element; print out on gummed labels; and even insert addresses automatically into individually typed, personalized letters. The search, sort, list, and insert capabilities of the word processor are impressive, and, except for its speed, mimic those of a larger computer. We find that its use has become essential in supporting and handling our large volume of correspondence and mailings to extension centers, experiment stations, and land-grant institutions.

A final application of the Lanier word processer is our agency newsletter, *Agricultural Libraries Information Notes* (ALIN). This is a monthly newsletter of agricultural library information which we prepare almost entirely on the word processor. It has an international distribution of over 2500 copies. Producing it, publishing it, and making sure it is timely is quite a task, but it is edited and composed by a staff of two people using the word processor. By typing ALIN in-house on the word processor, our production costs are greatly reduced, and our timeliness correspondingly enhanced. As a result, we have an attractive, inexpensive and timely newsletter of current library information. In addition, we may be able to send it electronically to a photocomposition machine in the department and eliminate another step—pasting up titles and headings, of which the Lanier is not yet capable. In the future we may also work out a way of automatically indexing the newsletter.

Online Information Retrieval Systems

When we first acquired a word processer, we did not fully appreciate or utilize its capabilities. But the idea came to us one day that, if the Lanier No Problem could communicate with other Lanier word processers, it ought to be able to communicate with other computers as well. The possibilities this communication would open to us for decentralized automated data processing seemed limitless. Word processers were springing up everywhere. If we could link them together, we could augment their power and capability with larger mainframe systems. A call to Lanier confirmed our hunch. Since the Lanier word processer uses a TTY/ASCII data communications format, the only problem was to reconcile the different computer dialects.

For several weeks we worked closely with Lynne Karsh, a Washington-based Lanier representative, who called all the computer centers with which TIS did business. She wrote separate programs for the Lanier No Problem for each incompatible communications dialect, rendering them compatible. The transmission rates and duplex switches had to be programmed. In the case of OCLC, the keyboard had to be modified to accommodate special keys, such as the backward slash key and the Display Record key. Once this programming was accomplished, and each system was fully tested, we had a set of tables (see Appendix A) which would turn our Lanier word processers into fully operational "smart" terminals. We could now communicate in an online mode with outside information retrieval systems, and store their output internally. We had, in effect, just doubled the value of our original investment. The only additional equipment necessary was a telephone acoustic coupler and the TTY/ASCII program available for purchase from Lanier.

The possibilities this programming opened up for us were tremendous. While working on a manuscript or bibliography, or researching a topic, we could now log into DIALOG and retrieve information from our databases (CRIS and AGRICOLA); store the output on Lanier diskettes; log off; further edit, merge, sort, or otherwise modify the citations; insert the results into letters; or store for further use. Assuming no copyright issues were involved (and they were not with our own databases), we could even retrieve several hundred citations, memorize them on the Lanier, and then mail the diskettes to another firm in Washington, D.C., which would process the citations further according to our own specifications and deliver to us camera-ready copy for rapid publication. The BOWNE Company experimented with us on this project, and offered valuable advice and programming assistance. Since the Lanier is able to communicate with other Laniers, we could transmit our search results to another word processer in another state or region and use the system for special delivery or electronic mail. We produced our first online bibliography using this new word processer capability when the Secretary of Agriculture wanted a search done immediately on the effects of volcanic ash on agriculture, as a result of the Mount Saint Helens eruption.

For those wishing to program their own Laniers for online searching, Lanier was kind enough to allow inclusion of their communications procedures and program instructions in appendixes to this paper (see Appendixes A and B). Included are tables for DIALOG, BRS and SDC, the National Library of Medicine, OCLC, and the two leading timesharing networks. You will probably have to ask your representative to interpret the tables, but should feel free to use the programs, as they are nonproprietary.

Conclusion

In conclusion, then, let me return to my original theme: managing complexity. Complexity is the very stuff of librarianship. But to manage it, we need both our minds and our tools. For a while, however, it seemed that we had lost control over one of our tools—automation. It seemed that automation was in the hands of data-processing specialists, and that we and our library operations were entirely at their mercy. Mechanization is essential to our work, but mechanizers seemed to be in control.

TIS has demonstrated that this need not be the case. By creatively programming word processers to perform small-scale automated data processing tasks, and by linking word processers to outside systems for larger assignments, librarians can regain some semblance of control over the automation process. Routine but complicated assignments necessary to provide management with information about the organization can be put on the word processer; numerous program activities can also be automated in-house. This frees the librarian for more important, and human, assignments. By linking word processers online with such default-driven language/systems as NOMAD, even larger automation projects can be accomplished, freeing even more the mind and imagination of librarians. And, all the time, the librarian is in command—not an outside computer specialist, program analyst, or systems designer. Once again, automation is in your own hands.

APPENDIX A

Program Instructions for On-Line Searching with Lanier Word Processers

```
                                                            USDA
02 00 00 03 02 00 05 00 2A 01 00 00 00 00 FF 01     NAL, Rm. 109
00 00 00 00 00 00 00 FF 00 00 00 00 00 00 00 00     Beltsville, Md.
E1 00 05 'LANIER TYPING ' E1 00 01
                                                    David Hoyt   344-3937

00 06 FF 19 FF 7F FF 1B 08 09 0A FF FF FF FF FF
FF FF FF FF FF FF FF FF FF 09 0B 05 11 FF 13 FF     DD/IRS (Direct Dial,
20 21 22 23 24 25 26 27 28 29 2A 2B 2C 2D 2E 2F        Information Retrieval Sys.
30 31 32 33 34 35 36 37 38 39 3A 3B 3C 3D 3E 3F
40 41 42 43 44 45 46 47 48 49 4A 4B 4C 4D 4E 4F     Lockheed
50 51 52 53 54 55 56 57 58 59 5A 5B 5C 5D 5E 5F     PRIME
60 61 62 63 64 65 66 67 68 69 6A 6B 6C 6D 6E 6F     Library of Congress
70 71 72 73 74 75 76 77 78 79 7A 7B 7C 7D 7E FF     Bibliographic Retrieval Sys.
FF FF FF FF FF FF FF FF FF FF FF FF FF FF 0F FF     Systems Devel. Corp.
FF FF FF FF FF FF FF FF FF FF FF FF FF FF FF FF     Control Data Corp.
FF FF FF FF FF FF FF FF FF FF FF FF FF FF FF FF     Federal CSS
FF FF FF FF FF FF FF FF FF FF FF FF FF FF FF FF     Juris
10 FF 04 FF FF FF FF FF FF FF FF FF 13 03 12        Medlars
0D FF FF FF FF FF FF FF FF FF FF FF FF FF FF
FF 0D 1A 17 18 02 09 FF 20 20 20 FF FF FF FF FF        REV. 2.1.1 TTY TABLE
FF FF FF 0J 06 07 0C 15 16 0E 07 06 FF FF FF FF        HALF DUPLEX
                                                       300  B/SEC
FF FF FF FF F7 1B FB FA 08 09 0A 1A F6 E1 F9 F8     NONE PARITY
FF 1C F3 1E F4 FF F5 FF FF FF FF FF FF FF FF FF     7 DATA BITS
20 21 22 23 24 25 26 27 28 29 2A 2B 2C 2D 2E 2F     1 STOP BIT
30 31 32 33 34 35 36 37 38 39 3A 3B 3C 3D 3E 3F
40 41 42 43 44 45 46 47 48 49 4A 4B 4C 4D 4E 4F     BREAK  - BREAK
50 51 52 53 54 55 56 57 58 59 5A 5B 5C 5D 5E 5F
5C 61 62 63 64 65 66 67 68 69 6A 6B 6C 6D 6E 6F
70 71 72 73 74 75 76 77 78 79 7A 7B 7C 7D 7E FF
```

APPENDIX A—*Continued*

```
02 00 00 03 02 00 05 00 2A 00 00 00 13 11 FF 01
00 00 00 00 00 00 00 FF 00 00 00 00 00 00 00 00
E1 00 05 'LANIER TYPING ' E1 00 01

00 06 FF 19 FF 7F FF 1B 08 09 0A FF FF FF FF FF
FF FF FF FF FF FF FF FF FF 09 0B 05 11 FF 13 FF
20 21 22 23 24 25 26 27 28 29 2A 2B 2C 2D 2E 2F
30 31 32 33 34 35 36 37 38 39 3A 3B 3C 3D 3E 3F
40 41 42 43 44 45 46 47 48 49 4A 4B 4C 4D 4E 4F
50 51 52 53 54 55 56 57 58 59 5A 5B 5C 5D 5E 5F
60 61 62 63 64 65 66 67 68 69 6A 6B 6C 6D 6E 6F
70 71 72 73 74 75 76 77 78 79 7A 7B 7C 7D 7E FF
FF FF FF FF FF FF FF FF FF FF FF FF FF FF 0F FF
FF FF FF FF FF FF FF FF FF FF FF FF FF FF FF FF
FF FF FF FF FF FF FF FF FF FF FF FF FF FF FF FF
FF FF FF FF FF FF FF FF FF FF FF FF FF FF FF FF
10 FF 04 FF FF FF FF FF FF FF FF FF 13 03 12
0D FF FF FF FF FF FF FF FF FF FF FF FF FF FF
FF 0D 1A 17 18 02 09 FF 20 20 20 FF FF FF FF FF
FF FF FF 01 06 07 0C 15 16 0E 07 06 FF FF FF FF

FF FF FF FF F7 1B FB FA 08 09 0A 1A F6 E1 F9 F8
FF 1C F3 1E F4 FF F5 FF FF FF FF FF FF FF FF FF
20 21 22 23 24 25 26 27 28 29 2A 2B 2C 2D 2E 2F
30 31 32 33 34 35 36 37 38 39 3A 3B 3C 3D 3E 3F
40 41 42 43 44 45 46 47 48 49 4A 4B 4C 4D 4E 4F
50 51 52 53 54 55 56 57 58 59 5A 5B 5C 5D 5E 5F
5C 61 62 63 64 65 66 67 68 69 6A 6B 6C 6D 6E 6F
70 71 72 73 74 75 76 77 78 79 7A 7B 7C 7D 7E FF
```

USDA
NAL, Rm. 109
Beltsville, Md.

David Hoyt   344-3937

TELENET

  REV. 2.1.1 TTY TABLE
  HALF DUPLEX
  300   B/SEC
  NONE PARITY
  7 DATA BITS
  1 STOP BIT

BREAK - BREAK
CTRL X - CTRL X

APPENDIX A—*Continued*

```
02 00 00 03 02 00 05 01 2A 00 00 00 00 00 FF 01
00 00 00 00 00 00 00 FF 00 00 00 00 00 00 00 00
E1 00 05 'LANIER TYPING ' E1 00 01

00 06 FF 19 FF 7F FF 1B 08 09 0A FF FF FF FF FF
FF FF FF FF FF FF FF FF FF 09 0B 05 11 FF 13 FF
20 21 22 23 24 25 26 27 28 29 2A 2B 2C 2D 2E 2F
30 31 32 33 34 35 36 37 38 39 3A 3B 3C 3D 3E 3F
40 41 42 43 44 45 46 47 48 49 4A 4B 4C 4D 4E 4F
50 51 52 53 54 55 56 57 58 59 5A 5B 5C 5D 5E 5F
60 61 62 63 64 65 66 67 68 69 6A 6B 6C 6D 6E 6F
70 71 72 73 74 75 76 77 78 79 7A 7B 7C 7D 7E FF
FF FF FF FF FF FF FF FF FF FF FF FF FF 0F FF
FF FF FF FF FF FF FF FF FF FF FF FF FF FF FF
FF FF FF FF FF FF FF FF FF FF FF FF FF FF FF
FF FF FF FF FF FF FF FF FF FF FF FF FF FF FF
10 FF 04 FF FF FF FF FF FF FF FF FF 13 03 12
0D FF FF FF FF FF FF FF FF FF FF FF FF FF FF
FF 0D 1A 17 18 02 09 FF 20 20 20 FF FF FF FF
FF FF FF 60 5C 07 0C 15 16 0E 07 06 FF FF FF FF

FF FF FF FF F7 1B FB FA 08 09 0A 1A F6 E1 F9 F8
FF 1C F3 1E F4 FF F5 FF FF FF FF FF FF FF FF
20 21 22 23 24 25 26 27 28 29 2A 2B 2C 2D 2E 2F
30 31 32 33 34 35 36 37 38 39 3A 3B 3C 3D 3E 3F
40 41 42 43 44 45 46 47 48 49 4A 4B 4C 4D 4E 4F
50 51 52 53 54 55 56 57 58 59 5A 5B 5C 5D 5E 5F
5C 61 62 63 64 65 66 67 68 69 6A 6B 6C 6D 6E 6F
70 71 72 73 74 75 76 77 78 79 7A 7B 7C 7D 7E FF
```

USDA
NAL, Rm. 109
Beltsville, Md.

David Hoyt   344-3937

OCLC and/or TYMNET

REV. 2.1.1 TTY TABLE
FULL DUPLEX
300 B/SEC
NONE PARITY
7 DATA BITS
1 STOP BIT

BREAK   – BREAK
CTRL C – CTRL C
BACKSLASH – BOTTOM LEFT KEY

DAVID R. HOYT

APPENDIX B

Procedures for Communicating with Computers

1. Turn system on; the switch is on the back left side of the system; flip it up. It will sound with a high-pitched tone. If it is already on, push the red button on the front and the system will sound.

2. Insert TTY/ASCII (yellow) program disc into the top disc drive with the label facing the ceiling and toward you; close door. Red light on disc drive will go on and off two times. Remove disc.

3. Insert "TIMNET" disc with the label facing the ceiling and toward you; close door. Give command:
FNC + L + DD/IRS, TELENET, *or* OCLC-TYMNET + EXEC
(Note: See last "tip" for which table to load!)
When red light goes on disc drive goes off, remove disc.

4. If you will want to print anything you are getting from any computer, insert blank disc. Anything to be printed must be memorized on disc first. This is explained in steps 9 & 10.

5. The screen will automatically default to 80 characters wide. If you need to change this: FRMT + H + width needed + EXEC
Set vertical to 26 lines: FRMT + V + length needed + EXEC
Clear margins: FRMT + K

6. To go into the communications mode: FNC + C + EXEC.
Format line will look like C----

7. You are now ready to dial up. When you get the high-pitched tone, place the phone in coupler. When the handset indicator on the front of the Lanier No Problem lights up, you have a link with the computer.

8. From this point on, you are on your own. Use the commands for whichever computer you are talking to.

9. If you are receiving from any computer and you want to print the data, you will have to memorize these on the Lanier disc first. Do the following:
Before giving the display command, set a memorize mode on the Lanier first:
CMC + M(memorize) + file name* + EXEC.
Format line will look like CW--M
After you have given your display command, DO NOT CARRIAGE RETURN. Erase your screen first: CMC + E + EXEC. This will clear the screen of whatever is on it. Then you can carriage return and the display will begin on line 1.

10. Since there are no printing capabilities using the TTY/ASCII program, you have to memorize the data on disc. To print out any information after you are done communicating and have signed off completely, do the following:
Remove all discs from system.

---

*This can be any name you want. It can only have twelve characters, none of which can be spaces or periods. Use slashes or dashes instead. Page will be automatically memorized when the vertical is filled up. To force the page to memorize if the vertical is not filled up, hold down the "down" arrow until you reach the vertical maximum.

APPENDIX B—*Continued*

Push red reset button on front of No Problem; it will sound the high-pitched tone again.

Insert blue word-processing program (Repaginate or List/Merge) with the label facing the ceiling and toward you; the red light will go on and off two times. Remove program disc.

Insert working disc that has material you want to print on it.

Give print command: FILE + P + name of file + spacebar + T + EXEC. Have paper in printer because the first page will print when you EXEC; put second sheet in printer and touch STOP/CONT. Continue until entire text has been printed.

Tips

To clear screen while in communications: CMC + E (erase) + EXEC.

To use Lanier for word processing while remaining tied to computer: FNC + O (online editor) + EXEC, use standard word-processing commands in this mode.

To go back to communications after using the online editor: FNC + C (communications) + EXEC.

To end communications after you have signed off of the computer: FNC + E (off-line editor) + EXEC.

To determine which table to load for communicating, find the database under the following table types:

LOAD DD/IRS (This stands for Direct Dial/Information Retrieval System)
    Library of Congress
    Prime
    Lockheed
    Bibliographic Retrieval System
    Systems Development Corporation
    Control Data Corporation
    Federal CSS
    Juris
    Medlars

LOAD OCLC-TYMNET
    OCLC
    TYMNET

LOAD TELENET
    When accessing any database but dialing the TELENET phone number.

W. DAVID PENNIMAN
Vice-President, Planning and Research
Director, Development Division
OCLC Online Computer Library Center

HOWARD TURTLE
Senior Research Scientist
OCLC Online Computer Library Center

THOMAS B. HICKEY
Senior Research Scientist
OCLC Online Computer Library Center

New Information Technologies and Opportunities Regarding Input/Output Devices

Introduction

This paper presents a framework for looking at different kinds of input/output devices, and provides some general characteristics regarding input/output devices currently on the market. A more detailed version of this paper appears as a chapter in the 1981 *Annual Review of Information Science and Technology.*[1]

This paper will cover personal-use input/output devices. By "personal use" we mean those things that would normally be found at a user work station to support individuals in their work activities. These devices would also make it possible for them to communicate with one or more information retrieval systems. Not included in this particular group are card readers, line printers, floppy discs, hard discs, modems, point-of-sale terminals (which you probably have contact with every day in supermarkets), and automated teller machines (where you can get cash any time of day or night).

Table 1 shows an outline of areas covered in this paper and in more detail in the *ARIST* chapter. The upper part of the table represents data-entry devices; the lower part represents display devices. Input devices include tactile, optical and other types, while display devices include hard copy, transient image and others. Before describing these devices in more detail, we will cover briefly something about the scientific foundations that are contributing to input/output device development.

TABLE 1
INPUT/OUTPUT DEVICES FOR PERSONAL USE

Data-Entry Devices		
Tactile	*Optical*	*Other*
Keyboards	Bar-code	Speech devices for the
Touch-sensitive displays	Optical character recognition	physically impaired
Other	Light pens	

Display Devices			
Hard-Copy	*Transient-Image*		*Other*
Standard paper	CRT	Flat panel	Audio devices for the
Electrostatic	standard	plasma	physically impaired
Electrosensitive	graphics	light-emitting	
Thermal	viewdata	diode	
		liquid crystal	
		display	
		electro-lumi-	
		nescent	
		other	

Source: Turtle, Howard, et al. "Data Entry/Display Devices for Interactive Information Retrieval." *Annual Review of Information Science and Technology*, vol. 16, edited by Martha E. Williams, p. 56, Table 1. White Plains, N.Y.: Knowledge Industry Publications, 1981.

Scientific Foundations of Input/Output Device Development

The traditional technologies or sciences that have contributed in this area include electronics, optics and magnetics. But the current trend in research has a great deal more emphasis on human factors, or, borrowing from our British friends, ergonomics. Also receiving emphasis is the psychology of working with a terminal. One area, for example, where psychology is playing a crucial role is in the study of eyestrain. Studies are being conducted of people who are using terminals for extended periods of time during the day, and particularly in the newspaper industry, where video displays are used a great deal. The major emphasis is being put on psychology by researchers, who are finding that eyestrain is not just a physiological phenomenon, but also a psychological one. The feeling is that the key to market success in the future with terminals (CRTs, keyboards, etc.) will really lie with how well the manufacturers can take into account the ergonomic aspects.

There are several professional societies associated with input/output device research. Those listed in table 2 are ones that we found quite useful in putting together the *ARIST* chapter. The publications of these societies were quite rich with information on terminals. As an example, the International Research Association for Newspaper Technology (IFRA) report series includes a great deal of information on ergonomics. The material on keyboard layout presented later in this paper is taken from one of their reports.[2] Also, the Institute of Electrical and Electronics Engineers (IEEE) and the Institute of Electronic Engineering (IEE) have extensive information that is useful. If you include publications of the Human Factors Society, the Ergonomics Society and the Society for Information Display, you can find out almost everything you want to know about data-entry and display devices, in terms of what is available in the published literature.

TABLE 2

RELATED PROFESSIONAL SOCIETIES

Electronics Industry Association
Ergonomics Society
Human Factors Society
IEEE
IEE
IFRA
Optical Society of America
Society for Information Display
Society of Photo-Optical Instrumentation Engineers

Also associated with input/output devices are a series of standards. We do have some standards in this area. Table 3 presents these in three major categories: communications standards, standards related to character sets displayed on these terminals, and the ergonomics (primarily the keyboard layout). A companion to this list is a list of organizations concerned with these standards (see table 4). At the international level there is the International Telephone and Telegraph Consultative Committee (CCITT). The American Library Association has standards on character sets. The IFRA is involved in keyboard layout and radiation standards. The government is involved via the National Institute for Occupational Safety and Health in terms of radiation levels for terminals. We would expect to see more standards coming out in the future with respect to terminals, particularly because there is going to be approximately a 20 percent annual growth rate in terminals over the next few years. With more and more terminals, there will be more pressure for standardization.

TABLE 3
Related Standards

Communications:
    EIA RS 232
    CCITT v. 24

Character Sets:
    ALA
    ASCII
    EBCDIC

Ergonomics:
    ANSI X4.14 (Keyboards)
    BS 2481

Source: Turtle, Howard, et al. "Data Entry/Display Devices for Interactive Information Retrieval." *Annual Review of Information Science and Technology*, vol. 16, edited by Martha E. Williams, p. 59. White Plains, N.Y.: Knowledge Industry Publications, 1981.

TABLE 4
Standards Information for Data Entry/Display Devices

American National Standards Institute
Electronic Industries Association
International Telephone & Telegraph Consultative Committee
American Library Association
International Research Organization for Newspaper Technology (ergonomics)
National Institute of Occupational Safety & Health
Occupational Safety & Health Administration
National Bureau of Standards
International Standards Organization

Source: Turtle, Howard, et al. "Data Entry/Display Devices for Interactive Information Retrieval." *Annual Review of Information Science and Technology*, vol. 16, edited by Martha E. Williams, p. 59. White Plains, N.Y.: Knowledge Industry Publications, 1981.

Data-Entry Technology

Table 1 shows tactile, optical and other types of data-entry technology. All of these are mechanisms by which you can convert some kind of mechanical or physical effort into a machine-readable form or an electronic form. The earliest form of data entry for computers was actually a series of toggle switches. It was not very user-friendly, except to programmers. Programmers were the only ones who were really interacting with the machine. Actually, this technique is coming back now. There has been some experimentation with a series of five keys that can be played like a chord on an organ. You can get many different combinations from five keys, taken *n* at a time. On most keyboards, however, each key corresponds to one letter and translates the mechanical movement into a binary electronic impulse. We do not think about that when we push the key for *A* or for the number *1*, but what we are really doing is nothing more than setting a series of toggle switches, as it used to be done in the older systems.

Keyboards, which are currently the most widely used data-entry devices, can be characterized by a number of features: the number of keys, the layout, the coding technique used (i.e., the way in which the user can look at the key and see what the key stands for), and the cost of the keyboard. Typically, a keyboard layout will have anywhere from 12 to 220 keys. The 220-key keyboard layout would be for something like the Japanese alphabet, and even that would not be the full character set. An example of keyboard layout variation is presented to us every day. The data-entry Touch-Tone key pad and an adding machine key pad perform the same function, yet are laid out differently. The Touch-Tone pad begins with *1* in the upper left-hand corner and moves to the lower right-hand corner. The adding machine goes from the lower left- to the upper right-hand corner. So even with something as simple as that, we have not standardized the keyboard layout yet. The "QWERTY" keyboard is the typical typewriter keyboard, having *Q, W, E, R, T, Y* in the upper left portion of the top alphabetic row. As far as the coding is concerned, the legends may appear on the keys themselves, and keys may have multiple legends appearing on the top and front surfaces of the keys. There can also be as many as two or three on each surface of the key. That can be quite confusing, and probably anybody who does not touch type must really search to find the symbols.

There has been some development work recently at Bell Labs on a virtual keyboard that projects symbols onto just the keys which need to be used at a particular time. Because a telephone operator may have a keyboard with several hundred keys on it, only the keys that need to be used for the next function are lit, and symbols are projected onto them from above. The next function that an operator performs may be different, so the keys will have different symbols projected onto them. This represents a very sophisticated "overlay" approach, with the symbols being projected onto the keys. A much simpler approach involves a small plastic template which is laid over a keyboard and has a set of symbols on it. This template can be changed to alter the symbols. Finally, the caps on each key can be changed so that special symbols can be placed on particular keys. In putting together a keyboard with function keys, for example, special caps can be placed on those function keys with the label indicating what that key is to be used for.

Costs of keyboards now range between $25 and $100 for the keyboard itself. Terminal manufacturers used to rely on custom-built keyboards, but they are now moving toward more standardized and mass-produced keyboards. This helps to lower the cost of keyboard data-entry systems.

Figure 1 shows by individual finger of the right and left hand the work load that currently exists for each finger using a "QWERTY" keyboard. The right hand has actually less work to do than the left hand. Furthermore, the distribution of work across the fingers is not even. Despite these shortcomings, this keyboard has been around for a long time. Figure 2 illustrates the results of some research reported by IFRA with a different keyboard layout.[3] This layout distributes the work more evenly between the two hands, and actually puts more work onto the right hand. One might think that definitive research had been done years ago, but because there are so many terminals and people are using so many keyboards this is only now receiving major emphasis. Years and years ago, when typewriters first came out, many of the keyboards were arranged in alphabetical order. We may see a return to that, because also being considered along with the layouts in figures 1 and 2 is the alphabetic key layout. Practically speaking, when you are using a one-finger approach to data entry, the keyboard might as well be arranged in alphabetical order.

As for other data-entry devices, there is the touch-sensitive screen used in computer-aided instruction, industrial control, and information storage and retrieval. It involves picking out a spot on the screen and touching it, and thus allows the user to have a virtual keyboard like the one being developed at Bell Labs, but in a simpler form. In this case, the keyboard is on the screen. A system designer can lay out a new keyboard on the screen as it is needed. The techniques used in this kind of touch-sensitive approach include a criss-cross of infrared beams, wire arrays or acoustical waves. Another approach involves multiple layers of some kind of conductive material. A unique voltage is generated at each spot of the screen that is pressed, so the system knows where the screen has been touched. These techniques are typically applied to a CRT or a plasma panel.

Other devices used for data entry are not quite so popular. These include the joy stick, which can be used to move the cursor, and is simply a small control lever. This device is used extensively in arcade games. It is also used in graphics, because it enables rapid movement of the cursor and represents a low-cost alternative to the light pen or to some other kind of touch-sensitive entry device. Similar to the joy stick is a mouse, which is just a little device that can be moved around on a flat surface. The device has a tracking wheel which indicates how far and in what direction it has been moved, and correspondingly moves the cursor on the screen in the same way. It is another low-cost alternative to the light pen. Finally, there is a digitizing tablet, which is somewhat like a touch screen, except that it has a much higher resolution and cannot be mounted over a display screen. It is used to locate something very accurately on a page. Its use is not as great in information retrieval as in cartography or where fine drawings are involved. An 8½"-by-11" digitizing tablet would typically cost about $1000.

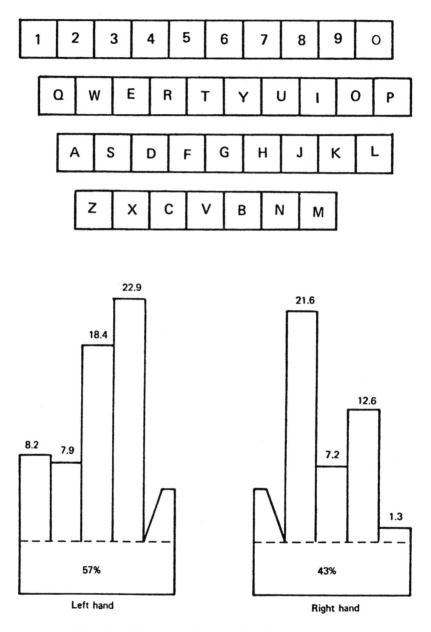

Fig. 1. The QWERTY Keyboard Layout and Workload Distribution

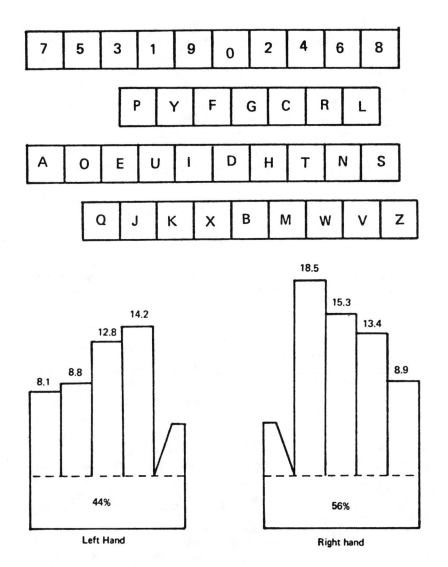

Figure 2

Source: Hart, David J. *The Human Aspects of Working with Visual Display Terminals* (International Research Association for Newspaper Technology Report No. 76/02). Feb. 1976. (Available from: IFRA, Washington Platz, 1-61 Darmstadt, West Germany.)

In addition to tactile entry devices, there are also other types of data-entry devices, the most widely used of which is the bar-code reader. It is used not only in circulation systems but, probably more widely, in inventory control systems. There are a number of different codes available, including Universal Product Code (UPC), Codabar and Code 39. These are all described in a 1978 National Library of Medicine report.[4] A bar-code reader typically uses either visible, infrared or laser light to sense the difference in hue and/or width of the bars and spaces between. Another type of device is an optical character reader, which is very much like a bar-code reader except that instead of reading bars, it reads a full character. There is an advantage to an optical character reader in that it operates on a human-readable image, but it also has a much higher error rate than a bar-code reader. Thus, there are tradeoffs, and the designer must decide what factors are most important for a particular application.

Light pens, unlike bar-code readers, respond to light rather than emitting it. Typically, they are used in conjunction with a CRT. The user touches the pen to a CRT, and the electronics of the device indicate where on the raster the pen was placed. In this respect it is like a touch-sensitive screen, and typically is used in graphics. It is also being used in information storage and retrieval systems where a menu-selection approach rather than a command-driven approach is involved.

There are other kinds of data-entry devices, such as speech recognition. While there is a lot now being said about speech recognition, practical applications are limited to a vocabulary of fewer than 250 words, and the device must be "tuned" to a particular speaker to be reliable. So while speech recognition has an exciting future, it is certainly a distant future. Also, there are devices with Braille keyboards that can be used by the visually impaired, and some work stations for quadraplegics are available at which programming and data entry can be done without the full use of one's hands.

Display Technology

The two basic approaches to data information display are hard copy and transient image. These approaches can be characterized in a variety of ways, including the manner in which the characters are represented. One method uses a matrix for forming a character, which is fast but not of print quality (unless the matrices are shifted and overlaid). Typically, a fully formed character rather than a matrix character is used for high-quality work, but is associated with higher cost and a lower print rate. Another means of characterizing display devices is by the method of printing. The two methods are serial (one letter at a time) and line (an entire line at one time) printing. Finally, display devices can be characterized by the kind of content to be printed, i.e., graphic and/or text.

With respect to hard-copy devices, one should consider the type of paper that is going to be used. Many printers use plain paper, particularly impact printers, which usually incorporate a fully formed character as opposed to a matrix character. Also there is xerographic printing, where a toner is bound to the paper through some electrostatic means; and ink jet printing, where the ink is charged electronically and adheres to the paper. There are also many hard-copy devices that use special paper—either heat-sensitive, light-sensitive, or electrical-charge-sensitive. Finally, there are some hard-copy devices that can produce color copies. At least three ribbons with three different colors would be required for an impact printer to produce a color hard copy. It is also possible to have multiple ink jets. Xerography can produce color prints as well, but it is quite expensive and not typically found at an individual work station.

Transient-image devices are very useful where no hard-copy record is required of the retrieval session. There are several advantages to transient-image output devices. They can operate at higher speeds, have lower purchase and operating costs, and are not as noisy as hard-copy devices. They also have lower maintenance costs and longer life, but they do have disadvantages. They are bulky, heavy and not easy to move around; they are more fragile than the newer hard-copy printing devices; and they operate at higher voltages. The most widely used transient-image device, of course, is the CRT which can be characterized by how the tube is scanned.

Raster scan means row-by-row, and is the most common method. Also found with some high-quality graphics devices is random scan or vector scan, typically used in very high-resolution devices. A CRT tube can be characterized as having low, moderate or high resolution. Low resolution, which we see when watching television, has 525 lines per screen. The moderate or normal CRT screen, used for most data input/output termi-nals, has 600-800 lines, with a 5 by 7 or 8 by 10 dot matrix. The very high quality graphic screen requires tremendously more storage than the regular CRT. It typically has a resolution of up to 4000 x 4000 pixels, or bits, on the screen.

The cost of a keyboard is $100 or less. The normal CRT cost is anywhere between $70 and $150. When these are packaged together, including the data-entry device, the CRT, the power supply, etc., the cost can be anywhere from $600 to $3000. For CRTs we expect to see a general cost reduction continuing, with color becoming more common and less expensive. There will be larger screens on the CRTs in the future, with improved resolution and increased intelligence via microprocesser technology.

In addition to the CRTs, there are other transient-image displays, including flat panel displays. These devices are typically compact and portable, with a character limit that is much lower than a CRT. One of the most widely used is the plasma panel which was developed at the University of Illinois. The plasma panel allows information to be projected via a rear screen projector in addition to displaying computer-transmitted information. Other types of flat panel displays include the light-emitting diode (LED), which is usually used for single-line displays. An LED is low in cost, operates on very simple circuitry, and is used extensively in small calculators. There is also a liquid crystal display (LCD) which, in many respects, is like the LED in terms of size and character capacity. Its physics are quite different, however, because it reflects light rather than emitting it. Therefore, the LCD works very well in bright light, whereas the LED may lose the image under bright light. Other device types include electroluminescent displays and audio-response systems. Texas Instruments has probably made the audio-response system most popular with a low-cost chip that is used in its game Speak and Spell. There are also output devices for the physically impaired involving tactile output and speaking terminals.

Table 5 shows how various input and output techniques are incorporated in user terminals today. Other combinations may be available, but this matrix represents what is typical in the marketplace. In many cases, more than one input/output technology is present in the same terminal. For example, it is now possible to find a CRT with a hard-copy printer built into it, instead of having a hard-copy printer attached to the side of it; a keyboard may have a joy stick or bar-code reader attached or built in.

Trends in Input/Output Devices

Finally, trends in the area of input/output devices may be divided for comment into two general areas: technology and applications. Improved technology will lead to lower prices. The less expensive terminals will be priced even lower than they are now. Some of the factors causing this decrease in price include annual reductions of as much as 40 percent in the cost of memory components, 25 percent in logic components, and 10 percent in communication components. Terminals that now cost just under $1000 will drop to under $600. There will be improved displays, and much more intelligence available in the displays. At the high end of the terminal line, where costs are $3000-$4000, there will be much more capability than is available today. None of these are fantastic predictions, but represent the most likely trends for terminals now and in the next few years. Do not look for use of voice data entry, for example, in the near future. Keyboard data entry and the CRT display will continue to dominate the

TABLE 5
COMBINATIONS OF INPUT AND OUTPUT TECHNIQUES IN USER TERMINALS

	Full Keyboard	Numeric Keypad	Touch Sensitive Display	Mouse/ Joy Stick	Graphics Tablet	Bar Code Reader	OCR	Light Pen	Speech Recognition
A. Input/Input									
Numeric Keypad	X								
Touch Sensitive Display	X	X							
Mouse/Joy Stick	X	X							
Graphics Tablet	X	X		X					
Bar Code Reader	X	X							
OCR	X	X							
Light Pens	X	X			X				
Speech Recognition	X	X							
B. Input/Output									
Standard Paper Hard-Copy	X	X							
Special Paper Hard-Copy	X	X							
Television	X	X		X					
Standard CRT	X	X	X	X	X	X	X	X	X
Graphics CRT	X	X		X	X			X	
Plasma Panel	X	X	X						
Speech Synthesis	X	X							X

Source: Turtle, Howard, et al. "Data Entry/Display Devices for Interactive Information Retrieval." *Annual Review of Information Science and Technology*, vol. 16, edited by Martha E. Williams, p. 72, Table 4. White Plains, N.Y.: Knowledge Industry Publications, 1981.

market; millions of these will be in use. Resolution will improve on display units; custom fonts and better graphics will be available. Stand-alone work stations, as used for word processing, will also be used as terminals much more widely. Because these units will proliferate, there will be a desire to link them together, and there will be more and more high-speed local networks, as well. There will be more touch-screen capability because of the increased public use of input/output devices. (Somebody can make a fortune marketing a liquid that cleans fingerprints off the screens of CRTs.) We can expect terminal installations to continue to grow at a rate of 18-20 percent in terms of numbers of terminals in the field. Terminals already outnumber typewriters in many offices. There will be more flat panel displays, particularly in the hand-held devices, whether they be games or computers.

As far as applications are concerned, it has been predicted that 30 percent of the homes in the United States will have some form of videotex terminal by 1992. Actually many of them already do (in the form of a regular television set), but we will start to see more and more videotex terminals, whether they use a standard television set or a special terminal. There will be greater use of electronic mail as postage rates go up; as a result, there will be more terminals for people who want to use the electronic mail capability. Teleconferencing will increase as travel costs rise. Teleconferencing involves not just sending words back and forth, but also sending graphic images, drawings, or pictures of yourself, so a person can watch you talk and also look at an illustration. We will see more special-purpose terminals for teleconferencing. Word processing will have a major influence on the terminal market, with its requirement for displays with much larger capacities than we currently have. These applications require the display of multiple pages on screens accommodating up to 160 by 160 characters.

Finally, there will have to be significant improvement in human factors, including keyboard design. We need a good virtual keyboard. Display devices that lend themselves to the use of multiple windows for displays will be required. With such devices one can arrange a display the same way he or she would arrange sheets of paper on a desk, or arrange three-by-five-inch index cards. We still have a long way to go in entry/display device development, but the market is there, and so are most of the technologies. The human factor will be the key to major improvements.

REFERENCES

1. Turtle, Howard, et al. "Data Entry/Display Devices for Interactive Information Retrieval." *Annual Review of Information Science and Technology*, vol. 16, edited by Martha E. Williams, pp. 55-83. White Plains, N.Y.: Knowledge Industry Publications, 1981.

2. Hart, David J. *The Human Aspects of Working with Visual Display Terminals* (International Research Association for Newspaper Technology Report No. 76/02). Feb. 1976. (Available from: IFRA, Washington Platz, 1-61 Darmstadt, West Germany.)

3. Ibid.

4. National Library of Medicine. Lister Hill National Center for Biomedical Communications. *Machine-Readable Identification Systems for Library Materials* (Lister Hill Contract Report CR 7801). Washington, D.C.: Lister Hill National Center for Biomedical Communications, 1978.

RICHARD H. VEITH
Manager
Video Information Systems
Logica, Inc.
New York, New York

Videotex
The New Information Systems

Introduction

Videotex and *teletext* are terms that are becoming harder and harder to define, and it is usually necessary to begin by explaining what the terms originally meant. Videotex has been used to refer to computerized information/entertainment systems using telephone lines to tie home television sets to computers. Teletext has been used to refer to computerized information/entertainment systems that send data to home television sets by encoding the data into unused portions of a television signal. At the receiving end—the television set—both videotex and teletext can look identical. And both, from the beginning, employed color and graphics as distinguishing characteristics.

However, both systems are still evolving technically and conceptually. Newer systems have been developed (for example, on cable television installations) which incorporate a little bit of both, as well as features of traditional timesharing computer systems. In many cases, the term *videotex* is used to refer to all of these systems that are designed to bring digital data to television sets or television monitors, usually using color and graphics.

Background

Since the 1960s, it has been recognized that the computer and telecommunications industries were overlapping more and more. Computer power has become widely accessible via telecommunications, and telecommunications techniques and methods have become computerized. Information services in the form of large online databases, both public and private, grew during the 1970s into worldwide systems offering access to millions, perhaps billions, of items of digitally stored data. This same general area of development also spawned such distinct services as Picture-phone (which dates back to at least 1930, and to a laboratory system in the 1960s) and two-way cable television (which was being tested by a dozen or so companies in the United States during 1971-74).[1] In fact, the first videotex system to gain recognition as such grew out of work in England on computerized reservation systems and on the British version of Picture-phone.[2] This first videotex service was initially called "viewdata" and later Prestel. At roughly the same time, perhaps even a little earlier, there also developed in England the first teletext service, which has been named Ceefax and is broadcast by the British Broadcasting Corporation (BBC). It is helpful, then, to review briefly the introduction of videotex and teletext systems in countries around the world.

Systems in Other Countries

This overview of systems in other countries does not attempt to be exhaustive. Teletext and videotex systems have either been developed or established in such countries as the United Kingdom, France, Canada, Japan, Sweden, the Netherlands, Austria, Switzerland, West Germany, Denmark, Finland, Australia, Hong Kong, and the United States.

The United Kingdom is recognized as the home of videotex and teletext, where the oldest commercial videotex and teletext services are in operation.[3] Teletext was tested in the late 1960s, and first became available on an experimental basis in 1974. Two years later, public teletext service began, with pages of text and graphics encoded into the unused portions of broadcast television signals. There are currently three teletext services available to anyone who has a television set with a teletext decoder. The BBC broadcasts Ceefax on BBC1, and Orbit on BBC2. The Independent Broadcasting Authority broadcasts Oracle as part of their television channel. During the same period, the videotex service known as Prestel was developed by the British Post Office, given a field trial in 1976, and has been offered as a commercial service since 1979.

As of early 1981, there are over 150,000 teletext users in the United Kingdom, and about 10,000 videotex users. (In Britain, after you get a suitably equipped television set, teletext reception is free, while videotex is not.) There are also about 350 users of the London-based Prestel International service, which is a videotex system designed for the international business community, and used by clients in seven countries.

France was probably the second major country to develop videotex and teletext systems.[4] In the mid-1970s, in a massive effort to expand and modernize their telephone system, France began what is called the "Télématique" program. As part of that program, a videotex system called Teletel was created that would permit access by users to the computer databases of any participating company. Unlike the Prestel system in the United Kingdom, the telephone company does not operate the computers used to store the data. However, one exception is the electronic directory service provided by the telephone authorities. This will be the first videotex system to be given a public trial, and will start during 1981.

The teletext system in France is called Antiope, although that name can also refer to the joint videotex/teletext designs produced for France. The initial teletext service in France began in 1977 and consisted of stock market reports broadcast on a television channel that does not carry a "regular" video program (thus, more scan lines can be used for data transmission). A public teletext service was started in 1979, and there are now about 1500 users.

Canada is the third major country to produce its own videotex and teletext system. The Canadian system, known as Telidon, grew out of work on the digital transmission of graphics. Thus, one of the distinguishing features of Telidon is the use of graphic instructions transmitted to a processer at the television set; only a few instruction codes are needed to tell the processer to draw a line, or a rectangle, or an arc, and so on. Telidon, as a name, can refer to both teletext and videotex systems. The Ontario Educational Communications Authority has been testing Telidon as a teletext service since mid-1980 with a small number of users. Also, nearly every provincial telephone company in Canada, and Bell Canada, has begun, or will soon begin, tests of Telidon as a videotex service.

Japan has also been developing videotex and teletext systems over the past several years. These systems are unlike the previously mentioned systems in that Japan cannot rely on a character generator built into the decoder in the television set (as the other systems do), because the character generator would have to be able to produce up to 3000 different characters. Instead, the Japanese system, called CAPTAIN, transmits the character patterns themselves for Kanji characters. Again, in contrast to other systems, CAPTAIN displays fifteen characters on a line and eight lines on a screen, while the previously mentioned systems display forty characters on a line and twenty to twenty-four lines on a screen. The CAPTAIN system has been installed on a trial basis since late 1979 and has about 1000 users. Japan has also tested teletext, dating back to 1978, and has conducted several field trials of teletext distributed via coaxial cable and fiber optic cables.[5]

Other countries, primarily in Western Europe, have also begun videotex and teletext services. In West Germany, Bildschirmtext has been available since mid-1980 and has some 6000 users. In the Netherlands, Viditel has 4000 users and has been operational since late 1980. Other countries with relatively small systems are Finland, Sweden, Norway, Denmark, Belgium, Switzerland, Austria, Italy, Spain, Hong Kong, and Australia.

Systems in the United States

In the United States the situation is rather complex, because there are many services that contain some of the features of videotex and teletext. Virtually any online database can be accessed via telephone lines and viewed on a television screen, particularly if the terminal is a microcomputer attached to a television set. The only difference between these services and videotex is the color and graphics (and possibly the fact that videotex, by definition, is supposed to be extremely easy to use). However, at least some of the online services are becoming easier to use, and some are adding color and graphics, too.

There are at least three online systems that are considered to be very close to videotex, primarily because they have sought users outside the traditional business and research communities. These three systems are: The Source, Compuserve, and the Dow Jones News/Retrieval Service. All three have designed their systems to be attractive to microcomputer owners, and have marketed their services in cooperation with one or more microcomputer companies. Dow Jones, for example, advertises its service in conjuction with Apple microcomputers. Compuserve has an arrangement with Radio Shack (the TRS-80) for joint selling efforts. The Source has been working with Texas Instruments (the 99/4). All three database services are also providing, or beginning to provide, color and graphics. The Source, for example, has announced a service called Texnet for owners of Texas Instruments' 99/4 microcomputer, which provides color, graphics and even sound. The Dow Jones News/Retrieval Service, available since 1977, has about 15,000 users; the Source and Compuserve have about 10,000 users each, and began service in 1979.

Other videotex systems have been developed by AT&T (currently being tested in Coral Gables, Florida), GTE (tested among a small group of companies), OCLC (tested in Columbus, Ohio), and the U.S. Department of Agriculture (known as the "Green Thumb" project in Kentucky), to name a few.

On the teletext side of the issue, KSL-TV in Salt Lake City has been testing teletext since 1978; CBS has been testing teletext signals in several cities since 1979; and Oak Broadcasting has been operating a trial service in Ft. Lauderdale, Florida, since 1980. Currently, teletext is on the air in Los Angeles (KNXT-TV and KCET-TV) and in Chicago (WFLD-TV and WGN-TV), and very soon will be also in Washington, D.C. (WETA-TV).

In the cable television arena, the distinction between videotex and teletext blurs considerably. Data may be transmitted via cables with or without being inserted into a portion of a television signal. And even if a television signal is used as the carrier, it could simply be a television-wide signal full of digital traffic. Tocom Inc., for example, a manufacturer of cable television equipment, has developed equipment that provides for teletext signals on fifty-five normal television channels, as well as data transmission independent of the television channels for polling and for limited interactive services. The Qube system, produced by Warner Amex, has recently begun testing the use of home microcomputers as a means of accessing existing online databases via the cable system. Mattel Electronics produces Intellivision, a stand-alone microcomputer for games and educational packages, that can also be used in a service called Playcable, where the games are stored at the cable head end to be accessed on demand by the home terminal.

To make matters a little more confusing, the satellite links among cable television systems have also been used for versions of teletext. Southern Satellite Systems sends a teletext signal (i.e., the data are encoded into unused portions of a regular television signal) carrying UPI and Reuters news to about sixty cable head ends, where the data are decoded and used to create a normal television picture of text and sent down the cable as a normal television channel. Time Inc. has announced that it plans to create a national teletext service using a television-wide signal full of data distributed via satellite to cable television systems. In fact, most major cable television companies have developed, or are preparing to develop, hybrid videotex/teletext services.

Conclusion

In summary, there are a great many companies in many countries striving to create a mass market for videotex and teletext. When the telephone was just getting started, it was not at all clear how it would be useful.[6] However, in a relatively short time, the business community found that the telephone could indeed be useful, and telephone systems spread, not only in business, but also into almost all homes. Similarly, videotex will no doubt be most successful first in commercial applications. But it will be only a matter of time before videotex and teletext services are mass-market operations.

As the mass markets develop, we can look for social effects similar to those associated with the growth of telephone usage. As the Harvard University Program on Technology and Society concluded, new technologies bring forth social changes "both to take advantage of the new capabilities and to deal with unforeseen consequences."[7] We are not yet able to see all the advantages, nor all the consequences.

REFERENCES

1. Veith, Richard H. *Talk-Back TV: Two-Way Cable Television*. Blue Ridge Summit, Pa.: TAB Books, 1976.

2. Fredida, Sam, and Malik, Rex. *The Viewdata Revolution*. London: Associated Business Press, 1979.

3. Several books describe the history of videotex. *See, for example*, Woolfe, Roger. *Videotex: The New Television-Telephone Information Services*. London: Heyden & Son, 1980.

4. *See, for example*: Bright, Roy D. "The Telematique Programme in France"; Termens, M. "TELETEL, The Planned Videotex Service"; Guillermin, J. "Development & Applications of the Antiope-Didon Technology"; and Maury, J.P. "Plans and Projection for the Electronic Directory Service." In *Viewdata and Videotex, 1980-81*, pp. 19-50. White Plains, N.Y.: Knowledge Industry Publications, 1980.

5. *See, for example*: Kumamoto, Takao, et al. "CAPTAIN Systems Features—Presentation Capability and Transmission Method"; Kimikazu, Yasuda. "Conception of CAPTAIN System—Background, Experiment and Future Plans"; Inoue, R. "The Index System of the CAPTAIN System Experimental Service"; Nobuo, Kurushima. " 'The Cooperative Association of Captain Information Providers' and Present State of Information Supply for the Experimental Service." In *Viewdata*, pp. 93-132.

6. Aronson, Sidney H. "Bell's Electrical Toy: What's the Use?" In *The Social Impact of the Telephone*, edited by Ithiel de Sola Pool, pp. 15-39. Cambridge, Mass.: MIT Press, 1977.

7. *Harvard University Program on Technology and Society: A Final Review*. Cambridge, Mass.: Harvard University, 1972, p. 7.

ADDITIONAL REFERENCES

Ferrarini, Elizabeth M. "Videotex: The Race to Plug In." *Computerworld* 15(18 March 1981), supplement.

"Videotex, Teletext, Viewdata—A Selected Bibliography." Washington, D.C.: National Association of Broadcasters, 1981.

J.L. Divilbiss
Associate Professor
Graduate School of Library and Information Science
at Urbana-Champaign

Telecommunications

The telecommunications industry in the United States is far larger than most people realize. To give some idea of its size, shipments of telecommunications equipment in 1981 totaled about $35 billion, and approximately 15,000 telecommunications professionals attend a typical trade show. The industry is characterized by brisk competition and a heady atmosphere of near science fiction innovation. My purpose here will be to highlight some recent developments that have particular significance for libraries.

Electronic Mail

There can't be many people left in this country who have not heard of electronic mail. The newspapers regularly report that Congress has or has not permitted the U.S. Postal Service (USPS) to proceed with various proposed electronic mail services. They also report that giant corporations such as AT&T, General Telephone, Xerox, and others are planning electronic mail services. Behind all this attention, however, there is considerable confusion about just what electronic mail is and what it will mean in practical terms.

Electronic mail is simply the transmission of messages from one human being to another through means that are partly or totally electronic. A telephone call is not electronic mail because "message" in this context implies that the creation and reception are not simultaneous. But if the conventional telephone call does not represent electronic mail, other familiar technologies do, including technologies in use for more than a century.

Facsimile

Facsimile is the transmission of individual images by electronic means. It was first demonstrated in 1843, and by the 1920s was in use in all large newspapers for wirephoto news. There were blithe predictions that facsimile would soon deliver the newspaper to receivers in homes, but that proved impractical, and the wirephoto remained almost the only use of facsimile until the mid-sixties.

In 1966, Magnavox and Xerox jointly developed facsimile equipment suitable for use in a business setting. This meant that small, inexpensive units which used plain paper could be attached to any telephone and could be used by untrained clerical help. This type of device has proved moderately successful, and there are more than 300,000 facsimile units presently in use. A few years ago, when grant money was easier to obtain, several libraries conducted studies to see if facsimile was practical for interlibrary loan work. To summarize, and perhaps oversimplify their findings, users were pleased with the improvement in delivery speed, but not so pleased that they would pay the additional cost that facsimile necessarily entailed. Librarians may yet make substantial use of facsimile, but only after facsimile costs are closer to postage costs.

The preponderance of facsimile units are used to communicate within a single firm or within a narrowly defined industry. For example, the coroners of Arizona are connected by a facsimile network. Ordinarily, all stations in such a network use the same kind of equipment in order to facilitate communication. On the other hand, when facsimile is used as a substitute for paper mail, serious problems of equipment compatibility arise. Two facsimile machines made by different manufacturers often cannot communicate because of differences in speed, resolution, modulation, encoding, protocols, and other technical factors. Thus, the facsimile unit is often regarded as a replacement for the interoffice memo rather than as a full-scale substitute for the U.S. mail.

As the pressure to abandon conventional paper mail grows, there is ample reason to believe that the problems of compatibility will be solved. First, manufacturers are attempting to maintain their competitive edge by designing versatile units that can communicate with other brands and models. Second, international standards organizations such as the International Telephone and Telegraph Consultative Committee (CCITT) have promulgated technical standards which are being widely adopted by facsimile manufacturers. This means, for example, that a facsimile unit designated as CCITT level II can communicate with any other level II machine regardless of brand. Third, facsimile networks exist to permit communication between incompatible units. The network solves the compatibility problem by receiving a message and computer-processing it to change the speed, resolution, modulation, and so on, before sending it on to the addressee.

Some types of technology are characterized by slow initial acceptance, followed by a period of rapid growth, ended only by market saturation. Black-and-white television is a convenient illustration of this. During the period of rapid growth, the more sets that were sold, the more profitable it became to build television stations. The more television stations that were built, the more attractive it became to own a television set. This cause/effect interrelationship continued until the market for sets was saturated, only to be repeated when color television was introduced. This might easily be the pattern of development for facsimile. The more facsimile units in use, the more beneficial it becomes to acquire facsimile capability. Facsimile units might be as commonplace as office copiers in a decade or so, depending, of course, on postal rates and the growth of other types of electronic mail.

On the other hand, many telecommunications professionals see facsimile as appropriate to only a narrow range of applications. Their argument is that the bulk of information transmitted electronically is in the form of text or tables of letters and numbers. For text, facsimile is dreadfully inefficient. A typical business letter that can take as long as six minutes to send by facsimile can be transmitted in character form in as little as eight seconds. The substantial differences in long-distance charges will favor technologies other than facsimile for routine business communication. Naturally, facsimile will always be used when pictures such as engineering drawings, fingerprints, advertising artwork, and the like are to be transmitted.

Communicating Word Processers

Throughout America, conventional typewriters are being replaced by word processers. It is simply the case that a $15,000 "smart typewriter" makes economic sense if it triples the productivity of $12,000-a-year typist. What does *not* make sense is to create a document on a $15,000 machine, place it in an envelope with a twenty-cent (as of this writing) stamp, and entrust it to the vagaries of the USPS. At least, it doesn't make much sense if the sender and recipient each have communicating word processers (CWPs). With CWPs, a completed document can be transmitted electronically and typed directly on the recipient's machine. This feature is sufficiently attractive that 90 percent of the word processers currently being sold have the communication capability, although only about 30 percent have the necessary communication hardware actually installed.

There are over 100 models of CWPs on the market, and this creates almost exactly the sort of compatibility problems seen in the facsimile field. Fortunately, the three solutions proposed for facsimile (more versatile machines, standards and networks) are applicable here, and there would seem to be no serious obstacles to the growth of this type of electronic mail.

Electronic Computer-Oriented Mail and Electronic Mail

The USPS has been aware for some time that facsimile, CWPs, computer-based message switching networks, and other forms of electronic mail are seriously eroding their first-class mail revenues. Their own projection is that 23 percent of first-class mail will move electronically by 1985. To counter this threat, the USPS has proposed an initial system, to be known as Electronic Computer-Oriented Mail (ECOM), which would be replaced by a much larger system known as Electronic Mail (EMSS). It is impossible to project with any certainty what form these systems will take, since the U.S. Post Office's action will be determined by Congress rather than by technological considerations. It does seem clear, however, that the rapid growth of electronic mail will force the price of first-class paper mail to levels at which it will be used only when electronic mail is not suitable.

Two-Way Cable

In many parts of the country, the typical home is connected to the outside world by two communication channels. The telephone company provides two tiny copper wires, and the cable television company provides a coaxial cable. For the information scientist, the important distinction between these two channels is that the CATV coaxial cable has about 100,000 times as much information transfer capacity as the telephone line. It has long seemed reasonable to exploit the great channel capacity of CATV for other than one-way transmission of entertainment television. Sensing this, the Federal Communications Commission in 1972 mandated "non-voice return" for all CATV systems. The exact meaning of this requirement was never entirely clear, and a few years later the Federal Communications Commission agreed that existing systems would not be required to add equipment for two-way transmission. All CATV systems installed since that ruling, however, must have the capability of permitting subscribers to communicate "upstream" or back to the head end of the system. Only a small number of CATV systems actually use the two-way capability at present, and they tend to use it in an unsophisticated way. Typically, multiple choices are presented on the screen, and the subscriber "votes" by pressing a numbered key.

Even though two-way CATV has not had a substantial impact yet, the potential for development is great. About 37 million homes in this country have access to cable (of those with access, only about one-half subscribe), and services such as information retrieval and electronic mail might gain wide usage if attractively priced. A good example of a multiple-use CATV network can be seen at the University of Illinois. CATV is to be installed in all residence halls. This will provide the usual entertainment channels and, in addition, alarm and monitoring systems, access to the University Computer-Assisted Instruction System, access to the computer system that serves the 3000 students taking programming courses in a given semester, and connection to the university's Library Computer System, which will provide access to some 10 million books at this campus and around the state.

The important point here is that CATV will often be installed for the entertainment channels; auxiliary services such as information retrieval will get a "free ride" on the facility, and hence may be attractively priced.

Digital Telephones

Many telephone users see only the most superficial of changes—the introduction of the Mickey Mouse phone—and do not realize that the telephone network behind that phone has been undergoing vast change. One of the most significant changes has been the steady replacement of analog transmission with digital.

In a conventional analog telephone system, the voice causes the diaphragm in the handset microphone to vibrate in the same way that an eardrum would vibrate. The electrical representation of this vibration is transmitted to the distant handset earphone, which converts the electrical signal back into sound. The major flaw in this approach is that, for toll calls, the electrical signal must pass through a great many amplifiers, each of which adds noise, cross-talk (portions of other conversations), and distortion. It is very much as if a document were copied on an office copier, a copy made of that copy, and so on for a dozen or a hundred iterations. Most of us have encountered "copies of copies," and can attest that this process cannot be repeated indefinitely if the results are to be useful.

In a digital telephone, the original speech vibrations are converted into a series of binary numbers that are transmitted to a similar instrument which converts them back into conventional analog form and then into sound. The information passing between the instruments is simply a string of bits represented in the form of electrical impulses. The striking advantage to this approach is that the amplifiers and switching equipment that process these pulses do not add noise or distortion. In principle, a digital signal can be transmitted through an unlimited number of amplifiers with no loss of fidelity. By way of analogy once again, a keypunch can be used to make a copy of a keypunched card, a copy can be made of that card and so on. If the keypunch does not break down somewhere in the process, the 100th "copy of a copy" will have exactly the same holes punched in it as the original.

The introduction of new telephone technology has always been controlled primarily by economic considerations. As an example, Touch-Tone sets are clearly superior to rotary dial telephones, but with an installed base of 50 million instruments, it simply was not possible to replace all the old telephones overnight. In a similar manner, digital systems are being phased in and will replace older equipment as quickly as economically feasible. The obvious advantage of digital phones is that connections of any distance will be totally free of noise, distortion and cross-talk.

There are very important but less obvious consequences that will accompany the introduction of digital phones. To understand how this new technology will affect data transmission, we must first look at how present-day telephone lines are used to connect computers and terminals.

Most telephone lines presently in use were designed a long time ago to transmit human speech. They do not work well with digital data, and for that reason it is necessary to have a modem between the computer or the terminal and the telephone line. It is the function of the modem at one end of a line to convert the digital information into tones that can be transmitted over a line designed for conversation. The modem at the other end of the line then converts these tones back into digital signals. For complex technical reasons, it is very costly to build modems that will convert digital data at rates above about 2400 bits per second (2400 bits per second is the rate used in the OCLC network, and represents 300 characters per second, or about 3000 words per minute of ordinary text). When higher data rates are essential, computer networks lease other specialized transmission facilities at costs much higher than for voice-grade lines.

With digital telephones, a quite different picture is obtained. The Bell System has standardized digital speech at 56,000 bits per second, the lowest rate that will ensure reasonable fidelity. This means that a digital instrument installed as a "telephone" might also serve for very high-speed data communication. A data rate of 56,000 bits per second is roughly the equivalent of 600 MARC records per minute. It may become commonplace to query remote databases, transfer large quantities of data in a short period, and then do detailed searching offline to minimize line charges.

The word *may* in the preceding sentence needs to be emphasized, because technological innovations of this kind can be enormously disruptive of rate structures. In other words, the Bell System presently offers 56,000-bits-per-second digital service at a price many times the price for ordinary voice-grade service. It may seek to offer digital telephone service in a way that does not undercut its market for specialized data transmission facilities. On the other hand, in the present climate of intense competition in the telecommunications field, it is simply not credible that a major technical advance could be made without a corresponding reduction in the price of service.

New Telephone Directories

The French PTT (the governmental agency that runs the post office, telephone and telegraph systems) has embarked on an ambitious plan to increase the number of telephones in France from 6 million to 14 million in the space of only four years. As part of its master plan, the PTT plans to eliminate all paper telephone directories by 1995 and so eliminate the printing and distribution of 100,000 tons of paper. It is its belief that providing a simple CRT terminal next to every telephone will be both cheaper and more satisfactory than the continued distribution of paper directories. The higher level of satisfaction would arise from the greater accuracy and timeliness of a computer-based directory. The "cheaper" aspect hinges on the expectation that terminals should be substantially less expensive in quantities of 14 million.

Trials of the new computer-based directories in Brittany have shown that more development work is needed before they can be installed throughout the country, but the PTT is moving ahead with the plan. Curiously, subscriber difficulties with the new system are rather similar to the problems experienced by users of computer-based public access catalogs. Designing inquiry systems that are simple but powerful, that accommodate the needs of typists and nontypists, and so on, remains extremely challenging. The French PTT has not found the job any easier than have designers of library systems.

If we assume that the French PTT eventually will install all those terminals, there should be some interesting ramifications: (1) very inexpensive terminals may be imported into this country, and (2) the telephone may be increasingly used as a substitute for paper mail. As an illustration, suppose you telephone someone who happens not to be in. Why not transmit a short, typed message that could be displayed upon his or her return? It seems likely that the PTT will encourage this kind of use, because in France, the post office does not compete with the phone company. In fact, the PTT has for some time promoted business use of facsimile, which naturally increases telephone revenue at the expense of post office revenue.

If the French experiment is successful, there should be considerable pressure for the introduction of similar technology in this country. It promises to be a bitter fight because the various parties—the Bell System, the USPS, the printing industry—have billions of dollars at stake.

Satellites

Almost forty years ago a science fiction writer described the concept of communications satellites in permanent orbit around the earth. The idea was generally viewed at that time as being about as loony as time travel. Less than two decades later, the Russians shocked the West by launching *Sputnik,* and the space race was on. By any measure, the communications technology that grew out of that race has been a whopping success. Last year the Federal Communications Commission authorized twenty new satellites, which certainly demonstrates that capitalists regard satellites as an attractive venture.

It is not just the launching of more and more satellites that makes this technology significant; satellites are getting bigger, and that will create a whole new range of applications. To illustrate, if you wanted to receive Public Broadcasting System programming directly from the WESTAR satellite, you would need a dish antenna approximately five meters (fifteen feet) in diameter. Such a dish is, naturally, expensive and awkward to install. The next generation of giant satellites will transmit signals so powerful that they can be received using a one-meter dish.* For technical reasons, the one-meter dish will also be suitable for transmitting *to* the satellite. I believe it is only a matter of time until there is a small dish atop the University of Illinois Library providing access to the OCLC network.

Conclusion

A paper dealing with recent developments in technology seems inevitably to drift from indicating trends and making projections into flat-out prophecy. And, of course, prophecies committed to print have a way of making the prophet look foolish. (Alfred Nobel predicted that dynamite was so terrible as to preclude future wars; Henry Ford predicted that the electric automobile would triumph over the gasoline-powered car, and on and on.) My predictions are only two, and to me they seem inescapable. The first is that every advance in telecommunications technology will further erode the autonomy that libraries have traditionally enjoyed. Loss of autonomy is not necessarily an unmitigated evil; it simply means that librarians will need to examine their goals and their resources, and separate the essential from the traditional. The second prediction is that the accelerating pace of technological innovation will make intelligent management of libraries much more difficult. There are many technically complex options open to librarians now—turnkey systems, networks,

---

*This might be called the Crosley Principle. Crosley sold inexpensive radios during the 1920s and 1930s, and when customers complained that they could not receive anything on their radios, Crosley responded by building the world's most powerful radio station.

public access catalogs, and so on—and the variety and complexity of these options is certain to increase. The librarian who is disdainful of technology will be left behind.

PETER B. SCHIPMA
Manager of Information Services
IIT

Videodiscs

To maintain a sense of perspective, I flavor my research activities at the
I I T Research Institute (IITRI) with the teaching, each semester, of an
introductory course in data processing. As illustrations in that course, I
frequently use science fiction stories, and it is extremely interesting to note
that those stories have a longer lifespan in the course content than most of
the factual material. The data processing field changes very rapidly. As an
introduction today, I'd like to quote from everybody's favorite science
fiction author, Dr. Isaac Asimov.

> At the present rate of computer advance, the time will soon come (always
> assuming our civilization does not crumble through our own folly) when
> any household can have a personal computer, with a complex and
> thorough-going system for information retrieval. This implies a number
> of things.
>   You can get what you need for daily life—weather information, the
> specials and prices at local stores, news and sports headlines.
>   You can get what you need for daily business—stock market reports,
> office data, letters received and sent out. You can stay home and still do
> your work at the office or plant, electronically, or even hold conferences
> by closed circuit television if your system is complex enough.
>   Most important, you can get information that you just happen to want
> for no other reason than that you want it.[1]

The good doctor goes on to elucidate the profound effects of such a society
on many aspects of life, principally that of education. You have already
heard of some of the new technologies that will affect the storage and
processing of information, and more are to come. The topic I will address
in this paper is that of videodiscs.

Videodiscs are a storage device for information, similar to scrolls,
books, motion pictures, or phonograph records. The medium itself is not

unlike the phonograph record, and videodiscs can be mass-produced by a stamping process, as are audiodiscs. In quantities of thousands, replicate cost is on the order of $2.00 each. The storage density is very high. An hour of television program material can be stored on one disc. So can the equivalent of 15,000 pages of text—that's about forty-five books (each at $0.045)!

A complete system requires not only the discs, but a display device, a playback machine, and a recorder to make the discs in the first place. Currently, videodisc recorders are very expensive, costing from $80,000 to more than $1 million. At this time, therefore, we speak of display-only systems; users would buy prerecorded material and own only the first three components of the system. The cost for these is quite low, since players cost about $500, and television sets, used for display, are only $200-$300.

The two major types of videodiscs are optical and capacitive. In both cases the very high storage density means that the information bits must be exceedingly small, measured in millionths of an inch, so they have to be formed by a laser beam. That is why the recorder cost is high. In the playback mode, there are large differences. Optical discs are read by a laser, but since no burning away of material is required, a very low-powered (an inexpensive) laser can be used. The MCA/Phillips disc is reflective, while that of Thomson-CSF is transmissive. For both of these optical systems there is no wear; only a light beam touches the disc, and a single frame could be played for years with no damage to the disc. The capacitive system, such as that recently marketed in the United States by RCA and announced in Japan by Japan Victor Corporation, uses a stylus, and is subject to wear. Also, because styli are large, compared to a focused laser beam, several frames are recorded on each of fewer tracks, and so frame play and single-frame search are more difficult to implement. Kodak, 3M and others are also working on other techniques for manufacturing videodiscs.

For consumer use, videodiscs offer the potential of lower-cost playback devices, lower-cost materials, and higher-quality picture over videotape. However, they do not have a recording feature, and that factor may outweigh the others in the movies-at-home marketplace. From the commercial information processing viewpoint, though, videodiscs are much more exciting than videotape. Not only can sequences be played through easily, in forward or reverse, at various speeds, without jitter or frame breakup (as with tape), but frames can be accessed randomly, on demand, either manually or under computer control, and any frame can be displayed for any length of time.

The optical videodisc thus has large advantages for use in educational activities. Costs are low enough to store huge amounts of material; any frame can be easily accessed; and much information can be stored on each disc. Whether or not the "television generation" will accept this technology remains to be seen.

It is costly to put material on videodiscs. Videodiscs will have to compete with both videotape and microforms, even though discs have some capabilities that cannot be matched by those media. In a recent cost analysis at IITRI, we found that the break-even point for discs versus microforms is about 250 copies. This strongly indicates that videodiscs are going to become a formidable competitor to current technologies. Other work at IITRI has led to the development of a system and methodology to store full text on videodiscs.[2]

Videodiscs are part of the revolution Dr. Asimov talked about. It is conceivable that, for a few thousand dollars, anyone could possess a library that Alexander would have given his empire to own. Just as each of us can have, at home, a music repertoire that couldn't be matched in a lifetime of concert attendance, one day each may also have an information collection rivaling that of most present-day libraries.

REFERENCES

1. Asimov, Isaac. "The New Learning." *Apple Magazine*, vol. 2, no. 2, 1981, p. 1.

2. Schipma, Peter B., and Becker, David S. "Text Storage and Display via Videodisc." *Proceedings of the ASIS Annual Meeting* 17(1980):103-05.

JEROME K. MILLER
Assistant Professor
Graduate School of Library and Information Science
University of Illinois at Urbana-Champaign

Copyright

There appear to be five basic systems employed to protect inventive and literary properties: patents, copyrights, trademarks, trade secrets, and contracts. Copyrights appear to have the greatest value for protecting computer programs and databases, but the other elements—patents, trademarks, trade secrets, and contracts—have some applications, or perceived application, to this area.

Patents have been a part of U.S. law since 1890. The patent law seems to be perfectly suitable for protecting an invention for a new mechanical process or a new chemical process, but it has not lent itself to the protection of computer programs. Obtaining a patent requires a lengthy legal process that commonly requires two or three years and an expenditure of a least a thousand dollars. Although the Supreme Court indicates that patents have some application to the protection of computer programs, the Court has rejected almost every patent application it has reviewed. The problem centers on the difference between algorithms, which the Court will not protect, and other aspects of computer programs which the Court indicates are eligible for patent protection. The first breakthrough in solving this problem occurred in a recent Supreme Court decision in the Diehr case.[1] The Court held that a computer-governed process for curing synthetic rubber was eligible for patent protection, but that the patent protection did not apply to the algorithm employed in the process. Other cases are pending which may open the way for patent protection for computer programs. At the moment, however, patents have little value for protecting computer programs.

Another form of protection for creative works is trademarks. Trademarks protect trade names, or service marks, such as the IBM name and logo, or the McDonald's name and logo. Trademark registration prevents a competitor from using these names or marks or anything similar which might mislead a consumer. Computer software producers may register the names of their programs, products or services, and the major firms probably have done so. Aside from the protection of names, logos or symbols, trademarks have little value for protecting software or hardware.

Trade secret laws are another means for protecting intellectual property or inventive property. The most famous trade secret is the Coca-Cola formula, which is known only to a few senior executives of the Coca-Cola Company. Unlike patents and copyrights, trade secrets have an indefinite life, so long as the secret is preserved. The trade secret law has limited application to programs, since a competent observer can examine a program and identify the new procedure or the new secret. Because secrecy is the essence of the trade secrets law, it can only be applied to specialized computer programs known to only a few people. Trade secrets in software, which is widely distributed to schools, libraries or businesses, have an extremely short life.

The fourth means of protection depends on contract law. Contracts are used to regulate the use of patents and copyrights by the licensee and to protect trade secrets. Contracts are also used to protect software which is not, or may not be, protected by copyright, patents or trade secrets. The importance of this tool has been enhanced by the confusion over patent and copyright protection for computer programs. The need for strong contract protection for software is somewhat reduced by the recent passage of the Copyright Amendment Act of 1980.

Copyright Protection

Copyright protection for computer programs has been a source of confusion for twenty-five years or longer. The problem stems from the term *writings* in Article I, Section 8 of the Constitution:

> The Congress shall have Power...
> To promote the Progress of Science and useful Arts, by securing for limited Times to Authors and Inventors the exclusive Right to their respective Writings and Discoveries....

The term *writings* did not cause any confusion in the eighteenth century when Congress extended copyright protection to maps and navigation charts, but it became a source of controversy as creators attempted to apply the copyright law to the newer media. Some interpreted *writings* literally, so as to deny copyright protection to works that were not created in an eye-legible form. This literal interpretation was embodied in the Supreme Court decision in *White-Smith* v. *Apollo* (1908).[2] In this case, the Court determined that player piano rolls were not "writings," so they were not eligible for copyright protection.

The limit on copyright protection for non—eye-legible materials was partially broken by the Copyright Amendment of 1912, which granted copyright protection to motion-picture films. It was further broken by the Sound Recording Amendment of 1971, which granted copyright protection to sound recordings. The question of copyright protection for non—eye-legible materials remained a source of confusion until the passage of the Copyright Revision Act of 1976. The whole question was settled very nicely in section 102(a), which states: "Copyright protection subsists, in accordance with this title, in original works of authorship fixed in any tangible medium of expression, now known or later developed, from which they can be perceived, reproduced, or otherwise communicated, either directly or with the aid of a machine or device."[3]

Although section 102(a) removed the old bugaboo about "writings," the act included a significant exception in section 117. Section 117 stated that the copyright law was to remain unchanged in regard to computer programs. Congress left the law unchanged since the National Commission on the New Technological Uses of Copyrighted Works (CONTU) was then studying the issue. Congress indicated that section 117 would be revised later to reflect CONTU's recommendations. The CONTU *Final Report* was issued in July 1978,[4] but its recommendations for changes in copyright protection for computers did not become law until December 1980, when it was attached to the 1980 Patent Revision Act.[5] Under the 1980 amendment, copyright protection for computer programs is provided under the general provisions of section 106.

Section 106

Section 106 contains the essential elements of copyright protection for authors, composers, artists, and the like:

§106. Exclusive rights in copyrighted works
Subject to sections 107 through 118, the owner of copyright under this title has the exclusive rights to do and to authorize any of the following:
(1) to reproduce the copyrighed work in copies or phonorecords;
(2) to prepare derivative works based upon the copyrighted work;
(3) to distribute copies or phonorecords of the copyrighted work to the public by sale or other transfer of ownership, or by rental, lease, or lending....[6]

The first two subsections are significant in that they give the author, or the author's publisher, the right to reproduce the work for sale or other distribution and to prepare new editions (derivative works). These exclusive rights are modified by the specific provisions of section 117 and the general provisions of section 107, on fair use.

Section 117

The new section 117, contained in the 1980 Patent Revision Act, embodies the computer program users' rights. The owners of copies of computer programs may make archival copies of programs. They are also permitted to make some changes in programs and to sell the programs and archival tapes. The text of the new section 117 reads as follows:

§117. Limitations on exclusive rights: Computer programs
Notwithstanding the provisions of section 106, it is not an infringement for the owner of a copy of a computer program to make or authorize the making of another copy or adaptation of that computer program provided:
(1) that such a new copy or adaptation is created as an essential step in the utilization of the computer program in conjuction with a machine and that it is used in no other manner, or
(2) that such new copy or adaptation is for archival purposes only and that all archival copies are destroyed in the event that continued possession of the computer program should cease to be rightful.
Any exact copies prepared in accordance with the provisions of this section may be leased, sold, or otherwise transferred, along with the copy from which such copies were prepared, only as part of the lease, sale, or other transfer of all rights in the program. Adaptations so prepared may be transferred only with the authorization of the copyright owner.[7]

Additional users' rights are available through section 107, on fair use.

Fair Use

The doctrine of fair use was developed by the courts to balance the interests of copyright proprietors and the users of copyrighted works. To simplify greatly, fair use permits persons other than the copyright owner to copy a small part of a work in a manner that is not injurious to the copyright owner. The doctrine of fair use was part of the common law of the United States until the Copyright Revision Act of 1976 went into effect in 1978. The fair use section is very brief, consisting of a broad definition of fair use and four criteria for applying the concept.

§107. Limitations on exclusive rights: Fair use
Notwithstanding the provisions of section 106, the fair use of a copyrighted work, including such use by reproduction in copies or phonorecords or by any other means specified by that section, for purposes such as criticism, comment, news reporting, teaching (including multiple copies for classroom use), scholarship, or research, is not an infringe-

ment of copyright. In determining whether the use made of a work in any
particular case is a fair use the factors to be considered shall include—
    (1) the purpose and character of the use, including whether such use is
        of a commercial nature or is for nonprofit educational purposes;
    (2) the nature of the copyrighted work;
    (3) the amount and substantiality of the portion used in relation to the
        copyrighted work as a whole; and
    (4) the effect of the use upon the potential market for or value of the
        copyrighted work.[8]

Although fair use has broad application, it is generally associated
with the work of students, scholars, teachers, and journalists. Although
little has been written about it, fair use also applies to the duplication and
use of copyrighted computer programs. Fair use permits the programmer
to include part of a copyrighted program in one he or she is writing. It also
permits the user of an online service to duplicate a portion of a copyrighted
database for the purpose of quoting it or including it in a new database.
Although the fair use section is useful, its application to computer programs is severely limited by the terms of the commonly used computer use
contracts. Because of the ambiguity surrounding patent and copyright
protection for programs, the owners of those materials have depended on
contracts to protect their interests. Although program or database contracts may not specifically forbid the application of fair use, their terms
appear to do so. Program users may be able to recover their fair use rights
by including an appropriate clause in their contracts, such as: "Nothing in
the terms of this contract contravenes the licensee's rights under Title 17,
Section 107, U.S. Code." The copyright owners may be reluctant to accept
this condition, but it may serve as an opening wedge in efforts to recover
the fair use rights embodied in the copyright law.

Input-Output

The two computer users' rights sections, sections 107 and 117, do not
address the question of entering copyrighted materials in computers. Some
persons have argued that they should be permitted to input copyrighted
materials and pay royalties when the materials were printed or incorporated in another work. Although inputting a very small amount of a work
may fall within the provisions of the fair use section, inputting more than a
small part of a work creates a copy "fixed in any tangible medium of
expression"[9]—and this is one of the rights reserved to the copyright owner
under section 106.[10]

Copyright Protection for Older Programs

The 1980 copyright amendment went into effect on the date of its passage, December 12, 1980. Neither the amendment nor the accompanying reports comment on copyright protection for programs created before that date. Until the courts rule to the contrary, it seems safe to assume that programs created before that date, and which display a copyright notice, are protected. Their protection appears to stem from the fact that computer programs are now a recognized and accepted media capable of copyright protection, and because the Copyright Office has been accepting computer programs for copyright registration since 1964. In 1964, John F. Banzhaf III, a law student, wrote a simple program which he recorded on a short length of magnetic tape. He wrapped the magnetic tape on a typewriter ribbon spool and submitted it to the Copyright Office for registration. After some negotiation with Mr. Banzhaf, the Copyright Office modified its procedures to accept copyright registration of computer programs.[11] The Copyright Office statement announcing this new procedure indicated computer programs would be accepted for copyright registration, but the Copyright Office could not assure the registrant that the copyright was legitimate.[12] The legitimacy of all those registrations accepted since 1964 was tacitly supported by the old section 117, which went into effect on January 1, 1978. It was further resolved by the Copyright Amendment Act of 1980, which provided full copyright protection for computer programs. Although the copyright acts of 1976 and 1980 are not retroactive and the law has not been tested in the courts, one may assume that all of those copyrights created from 1964 to 1978 are protected under the terms of the 1909 act, and that they would be respected by the courts. It may be interesting to note that IBM holds over half of the copyrights registered under the 1964 procedure. In hindsight, it appears that IBM legal staff made a good decision to register those programs to assure their protection.

Some software vendors took an alternate approach to copyright protection. They issued all of their programs with a copyright notice, but they did not register the copyrights. Their copyrights are probably valid under the terms of the 1909 act, the 1976 act, and the 1980 amendment. Since the copyright proprietors did not register their programs, they probably will not receive the full benefit of copyright protection, as registration is essential to obtain some benefits. One should not assume that their copyrights are invalid, but it may be unprofitable for a proprietor to sue an infringer.

Are Databases Programs?

A final question concerns the application of the 1980 copyright amendment to bibliographic databases. The 1980 amendment offers the following basic definition of the materials covered by the amendment: "A 'computer program' is a set of statements or instructions to be used directly or indirectly in a computer in order to bring about a certain result."[13] The CONTU *Final Report* seems to suggest that databases are covered by that definition, but many question whether that definition is broad enough to cover databases.[14] Although the CONTU *Final Report* does not have the force of law, it seems safe to assume that it is an accurate reflection of the intent of the legislators who accepted the CONTU recommendations and embodied them in the copyright law.

The key question, however, is not whether databases fall within the definition of computer programs, but whether or not they fall within the definition of a compilation:

> A "compilation" is a work formed by the collection and assembling of preexisting materials or of data that are selected, coordinated, or arranged in such a way that the resulting work as a whole constitutes an original work of authorship. The term "compilation" includes collective works....
>
> A "collective work" is a work, such as a periodical issue, anthology, or encyclopedia, in which a number of contributions, constituting separate and independent works in themselves, are assembled into a collective whole.[15]

If static or dynamic databases fall within either of those definitions, they are eligible for copyright protection. In such a case, the copyright protection extends only to "the material contributed by the author of such work, as distinguished from the preexisting material employed in the work, and does not imply any exclusive right in the preexisting material."[16] Under these terms, copyright protection for a database consisting of some new materials and some materials obtained from other sources is limited to the materials and organization supplied by the creator. If some of the materials in the database are in the public domain (e.g., catalog copy prepared by the Library of Congress), then they remain in the public domain. If some of the materials in the database are taken from a copyrighted source (e.g., a bibliographic citation from a Bowker or Wilson index), then the copyright in that citation remains the property of the original copyright holder. Under these conditions, it may be difficult to sort out the ownership of all of the data in a database, but there is little doubt that copyright protection is available for these databases.

Copyright Registration and Notices

The registration and notice requirements were originally designed for items that were finished and registered before they entered the market. Programs and databases may be in a constant state of change and that raises questions about the best procedures for providing full copyright protection for them. The CONTU *Final Report* suggests that a procedure should be established by the Copyright Office to facilitate occasional updating of these registrations.[17] Until the Copyright Office provides appropriate procedures for updating registrations, it seems appropriate to register these products as early as possible. When procedures are established to handle this material, the copyright owners will probably have to provide supplementary registration from time to time.

Copyright notices are not difficult to provide. A notice containing the word *copyright* or the © symbol, the name of the copyright owner, and the year of creation should appear on the printout or on the screen each time the program or database is applied or accessed. Additional dates should be added to the notice for each year in which the program or database is revised or expanded (e.g., Copyright East-West Data Service, 1978, 1979, 1980, 1981, 1982). Notices also should appear on programming sheets, program guides, and the like.

Conclusion

Copyright protection for computer programs and databases has been a source of confusion for over twenty years. The confusion over the term *writings* in the Constitution was an early bar to copyright protection for the electronic media. The problem was overcome through the broad terms of the Copyright Revision Act of 1976, but that act contained one section freezing copyright protection for computer programs until the recommendations of the National Commission on New Technological Uses of Copyrighted Works could be implemented. The commission completed its work in 1978, and an amendment to the Copyright Revision Act of 1976, embodying its recommendations, was passed in December 1980. This removed the section freezing copyright protection for computer programs, thereby allowing the general provisions of the act to apply to computer programs as they apply to books, films, records, and other media. The 1980 amendment went beyond removing the freeze on copyright protection for computer programs; it also provided a reasonable set of users' rights to facilitate revising and making archival copies of programs.

Many of the questions about inputting copyrighted materials, and copyright protection for dynamic databases, have been resolved by the 1980 amendment. Other questions about registration and deposit procedures are still unanswered, but the resolution of these problems will not require legislation. The Copyright Office can handle those matters through its rule-making authority, and it will probably do so in the near future. In short, most of the problems in the application of the copyright law to computer programs and databases have been resolved, although the answers will not please everyone.

REFERENCES

1. Sidney A. Diamond *v.* James R. Diehr II (S.C. 79-1112). In *BNA's Patent, Trademark and Copyright Journal*, no. 519 (5 March 1981), pp. D.1—D.12.

2. White-Smith *v.* Apollo, 209 *U.S. Reports* 1; 28 S. Ct. 319 (1908).

3. *U.S. Code*, Title 17, "Copyrights," sec. 102(a). (Hereinafter cited as Copyright Act.)

4. National Commission on New Technological Uses of Copyrighted Works (CONTU). *Final Report.* Washington, D.C.: USGPO, 1978.

5. P.L. 96-517, "An Act to Amend the Patent and Trademark Laws." 12 Dec. 1980. U.S. *Statutes at Large*, vol. 126, sec. 10, p. 3028.

6. Copyright Act, sec. 106.

7. Title 17, "Copyrights." *U.S. Code Annotated, 1980 Laws Special Pamphlet*, pt. 1, sec. 117.

8. Copyright Act, sec. 107.

9. Ibid., sec. 102(a).

10. Ibid., sec 106(1).

11. Banzhaf, John F. "Copyright Protection for Computer Programs." In *The Law of Software* (Proceedings of the First Annual Conference on the Law of Software, 1968). Washington, D.C.: George Washington University, 1968, pp. C-33—C-50.

12. U.S. Copyright Office. "Computer Programs" (Circular 61). Washington, D.C.: 1974.

13. Copyright Act, sec. 101.

14. CONTU, *Final Report*, pp. 94-96.

15. Copyright Act, sec. 101.

16. Ibid., sec. 103(b).

17. CONTU, *Final Report*, p. 96.

BRIAN NIELSEN
Head, Reference Department
Northwestern University Library
Evanston, Illinois

Technological Change
and Professional Identity

What I will present here consists of a number of seemingly disparate trails of thinking that I have been pursuing for the past four years or so. Charting those trails on a single map, relating technological change in the information world to the ongoing history of librarianship, as well as to larger managerial and social issues, is what I hope is accomplished in this paper.

I would like to start by introducing an image of this conference as a whole, and a series of alternative images of my place as the last spot on the program. It is the image of a technological feast. I think it will illustrate the underlying rationale with which I undertook this paper. First picture the program, up to now, as a great smorgasbord of technological pickles, side dishes and main courses, with the audience invited to fill their plates. There they are, the tempting relishes (microcomputers, mmmmmm), hearty pastas (word processors and telecommunication devices), and flashy ice-sculpture salad arrangements (videotex and disc), along with the varieties of bread and butter (micrographics and input/output devices). All are arranged attractively to the eye, and in as convenient a form as possible, to encourage the diners to eat heartily.

After having conjured up this image, where, I asked myself, do I fit in? My first thought was obvious—dessert. At the end of the table, I am the last item to maneuver onto the already overloaded plate—if you go in for desserts. Some, of course, have already left the table and gone off somewhere to sit down and eat. These are either the practical-minded, no-nonsense eaters to whom sociological musing is most definitely a frill, or the virtuous dieters making their way home after too many days out of their libraries. To those still left, out of either politeness or a true love for the pastry that will round out an already rich meal: hold back your compliments to the chef. No, I decided that image would not work; not dessert. People who go in for sociology may often be pretty sour—they have a reputation for enjoying making other people uncomfortable—and a number of them have been found by many to be, for one reason or another, completely indigestible. The dessert image just did not fit. I had to devise something else to get a sense of my function on the program.

My next thought was busboy. Here I am, sweeping up after the smorgasbord, trying to create some order following the disarray of the feast. There is a certain amount of plate-scraping—to deal with those messy issues that did not get fully dealt with (like how to pay for all that technology). Maybe I will have to make some clatter to help ease the last diners out, with some bold pronouncement about the future of the tree with the decline of paper. But I will have to watch out for those sharp knives and forks of criticism, for as an academic and a fairly traditional library practitioner, I have some vulnerabilities: I do not have a degree in electrical engineering, I have never mounted a disc pack, and I have never had to meet a payroll. Still, the busboy image does not really suit me either, for the busboy is silent; he has no direct contact or identification with the diners.

What I have finally settled on as an image is something more anthropomorphic than a dessert, something a bit more dignified than a busboy. What I will be today is a restaurant critic, a literate and dispassionate commentator on the feast served to the library world by the information technologists. As a restaurant critic I have an obligation to be honest about my personal tastes in food. But I also must be sensitive to my readership, to be certain to cover such essential details as ambience and price. Today I will even go beyond that a bit, and discuss nutritive value. To achieve such balance in critical perspective, there is no better Michelin guide to emulate than that provided by sociology—a field that, to me at least, goes further than any other humanistic area of study in bringing understanding to the issues we face as librarians in a technological age.

To help my audience pursue the thread of argument that runs through this paper, I would like, at this time, to provide a brief outline of that argument. A key to understanding librarianship's relationship to technological adoption is to develop a more disinterested model of what librarianship is. The commonly accepted model in the occupation currently is the classic "attribute" model of professionalism. After reviewing the classic professional attribute model, I will present an alternative model of how professions behave. This model is now widely accepted and used by sociologists, and is known as a "process" or "conflict" model. An important element of the process model is the idea of occupational segments, developed in a seminal paper by Rue Bucher and Anselm Strauss,[1] which I will briefly recap. With this process model of professions in mind, I will then look specifically at librarianship. It is my thesis that technology has always played a critical role in the "process" of librarianship, and that today this role is expanding at the expense of other social values which librarianship pursued in the past. I will offer a number of arguments showing the status benefits to librarianship which advanced technology brings, and explore in some depth the consequences of librarianship's increasing reliance on technical solutions. Through a more critical examination of the social ends to which new technologies are being put, I hope to persuade librarians to take full cognizance of their responsibilities in the information world. I wish to make explicit some of the value choices made by librarians that now seem partially hidden, and through that urge a more general examination of the values implicit in much technological decision-making. Only through such higher-level perspectives on decision-making as they are shared by many librarians, in a manner respectful of a diversity of interests, can we hope to avoid the institutionalization of information systems which run counter to human needs. Having now provided a general outline for my remarks, I will proceed with an examination of two competing models of a profession, during which I hope to demonstrate that one is superior to the other in terms of objectivity and accuracy.

Virtually all of us who have gone through library school and have endured a course on "the library in society" have doubtless heard the time-honored lecture on professionalism. That lecture, usually titled "Is Librarianship a Profession?" (or among the bolder, like Melvil Dewey's own "librarianship *is* a profession"[2]), typically reviews a canned definition of professionalism and then proceeds to point out how well librarianship fits the definition. The definition used has been around with only minor variations at least since 1915 when Abraham Flexner argued the case for social workers,[3] and the classic statement of it is generally considered the one by Greenwood.[4] Central to this definition is its logic of assigning professional status to an occupation based on specific traits or attributes of that occupation. Criterion attributes for professional status include such things as the occupation having a scientific or specialized and esoteric knowledge base, an orientation toward service to the public, an extended period of training required for entry, a code of ethical conduct, and a professional association. This model is widely taught not only in library schools, but also in many other programs, such as schools of nursing and journalism, or wherever professional status is an issue.

The attribute model has long been troublesome to sociologists, and has gradually been replaced by models which are more sophisticated. There is one great problem with the attribute model, which is this: since "professional status" is defined solely in terms of attributes, the model has promulgated the popular notion that if an occupation wants "professional status," all the occupation need do is strive to achieve all the attributes it can.[5] Thus, undertakers can develop codes of ethics, copywriters can form professional associations, chiropractors can require bachelor's degrees for entry into chiropractic schools, and so on—which is, in effect, the creation of the form, without necessarily any substance, of professionalism. Librarianship, too, of course, in its striving for greater social recognition, has worked to achieve such attributes as are called for in the attribute model of professionalism. The recent effort within ALA to promulgate a meaningful code of ethics is just one example. The attribute model, then, rather than being an objective definition of anything, is a set of ideas used by certain occupations to get what they want—a special type of social recognition called "professional." Some sociologists have gone so far in rejecting the attribute model as to call the terms *professionalism* and *profession* "folk concepts," having no relevance to sociological scholarship at all.

What has replaced the attribute model as a sociological tool to better understand those occupations which call themselves professions? No single simple, alternative model has yet been precisely codified, but there is general agreement that the *actions* or *moves* an occupation engages in to achieve or maintain a high social status are more important to study than whether some set level—"professional"—has been achieved or not achieved. Such an agreement avoids the pitfall of having sociologists make some judgment as to whether or not an occupation is a profession, since in reality that judgment has relatively little, if any, meaning. What does have meaning, of course, is the *belief* common within certain occupations that professional status is a desirable goal. Such a belief is a reliable predictor of certain actions designed to achieve the goal of professional status. This refocusing of attention away from the spurious issue of whether an occupation is or is not a profession, and toward an examination of action to achieve the imputed goal, is called a "conflict" or "process" approach to the study of occupations.

An important theoretical building block in developing this more objective approach was provided in a 1961 paper called "Professions in Process" by Rue Bucher and Anselm Strauss, which was published in the *American Journal of Sociology*.[6] Bucher and Strauss drew attention to the means by which professions sustain a high social status, but more importantly, they pointed out that to conceive of an occupational group as a unified and homogeneous "profession" was to ignore a lot of the significant variation within the group. They developed the concept of professional "segments," subgroups within the occupation as a whole which have varying, and sometimes conflicting, interests. These segments may be specialties, they may be special roles designed to perform public relations for the occupational group, or interest groups bent on making certain changes in the occupation as a whole. The paper defined professions in a new way: "as loose amalgamations of segments pursuing different objectives in different manners and more or less delicately held together under a common name at a particular period in history."[7] These segments, the authors argued, behave much like political movements, in which there may be strong leaders, competing ideologies, jockeying for special recognition and influence with the public at large, and other activities that belie the sense of "professional unity" that is assumed whenever we generalize about an occupation as a whole. The idea that certain occupations could be analyzed in terms of the actions of segments was an important contribution to the process model of professionalism. What I shall present here, relating technological change to the professionalization of librarianship, relies heavily on the concepts that Bucher and Strauss developed.

Bucher and Strauss outline a rather extensive typology of how occupational segments can be studied, using examples from medicine that are familiar to all of us; but three research propositions they discuss are particularly important to my purposes here. First, they note the special problems posed by recruitment into occupations, by which they are referring to how professional schools turn out the "right kind" of new professionals. Schools, they note, can be a "critical battleground" upon which differing interests within a profession fight to gain new recruits for one segment or another.[8] Second, the authors note that segments often are organized around some "core task" and seek recognition of that task by other segments and by the lay world as elemental to the profession as a whole. For the medical field, the most prominent "core task" has historically been the doctor-patient relationship, although, of course, many physicians do not participate in that task to any significant degree in their workday—witness pathologists, medical researchers and administrators, and radiologists, for example.[9] Third, recognizing that homogeneity in a profession is illusory, yet important for the occupation's relationship with the lay world, Bucher and Strauss call attention to what they refer to as "spurious unity and public relations." In this context, allow me to quote briefly a comment they make about professional associations: "It seems that associations must be regarded in terms of just whose fateful interests within the profession are served. Associations are not everybody's association but represent one segment or a particular alliance of segments. Sociologists may ask of medicine, for example: Who has an interest in thinking of medicine as a whole, and which segments take on the role of spokesmen to the public?"[10] These three research propositions—recruitment battles in professional schools, the definition of "core tasks," and "spurious unity and public relations"—suggest ways of looking at occupational segments as they maneuver among one another for a larger piece of the status pie.

Having sketched out what I believe is a more fruitful way to describe the activities of certain occupational groups, I would like to consider how a process model may be used to examine librarianship. It should be clear from my synopsis of the process perspective that I am definitely not interested in arguing the question of whether librarianship is a profession or not. I *am* interested in the continued actions taken by librarians, singly and in groups, to maintain or enhance their group status within librarianship.

My central thesis is that new information technologies are serving as powerful tools, not just in what they do in physical terms of moving information around, but as social instruments in the hands of certain occupational segments. Like the white lab coat of the scientist or the stethoscope of the doctor, information technologies have social communicative value quite apart from their manifest functions. The particular end to which new technologies are especially suitable as means is the acquisition of professional attributes.

Let us first look at the value of new technologies for the professionalization of librarianship in the context of the recruitment conflicts suggested by Bucher and Strauss. Library schools have long been under pressure, at least since the Williamson Report of 1923,[11] to provide a more scientific base to the content of their instruction. This pressure came from a variety of sources, one of them being the university community's perception that what was being taught in library schools was not sufficiently rigorous to merit graduate school status. Another pressure came from the strong drive for professionalization from many occupational segments, since attainment of professional status requires a scientific and continually growing knowledge base.

The most significant early response to that pressure for more science was the attempt to forge a social science knowledge base for librarianship at the University of Chicago in the 1930s. Douglas Waples's reading interest studies, Dean Wilson's library surveys, and Bernard Berelson's social/political analysis of the public library were among the attempts made to create a social science of librarianship.[12] Counterpressure from the field prevented the social science-based definition of library science from gaining a lasting foothold. Then, following World War II, the development of operations research and kindred methodologies brought the hope that such mathematical techniques could serve to build the knowledge base librarianship needed. The problem which advocates of the operations research movement had was that the length of training required to master that area was substantial; thus, very few mathematically-oriented researchers were ever recruited to build a significant movement. And, like the social science movement before it, operations research could not attain the support of a sufficient number of practitioners in the field because application just seemed so difficult.

But postwar technology was different. Though technology is not "science," twentieth-century technologies related to elemental electronic or other physical processes are closely wedded in the public mind with science. The library world was in a fortunate position to benefit from that public perception, especially following the publication of Vannevar Bush's "As We May Think"[13] and the interest of a number of early computer specialists in word processing. Computer research had immediate legitimacy on the university campus. Although the early librarian "information science" advocates of computer application had over a ten-year fight with library schools to bring computers into the curriculum, it is safe to say at this point that they have won. The requests from library school deans to senior university administrators for more terminals, more computer power, more electronic hardware of all sorts, legitimizes the professional status of library schools in the eyes of the academic community as nothing before ever did. Other equipment requests that had been made in the past, such as for media hardware, provided no such benefit because of their unfortunate association with elementary and secondary education.

In addition to this clear legitimation benefit that computer technology provided library education, there is another benefit to library educators faced with curriculum development problems. Teaching about new technologies is an easy way to keep a course "current," much easier than organizing a course around new research findings in our field. Developing a course around new technologies is likely much more satisfying to students because the course is clearly "relevant," to use the overworn word of the sixties. This strategy for curriculum design also wins friends among practitioners for the same reason. Never mind that most of what would be learned in such a course likely will be fairly meaningless in five years as still newer and better gadgets come along; still the students are happy, they earn their course credit, and once they pick up their sheepskins they are no longer the school's problem. Instead of teaching students to think, it is easier just to keep them busy and then leave them to that great new panacea, "continuing education."

To summarize the points made here about the recruitment conflicts evident in library education, we can see that new technologies appear to create new "knowledge"—in actuality, merely new "know-how"—which increases the promise for professional status that librarianship seeks. Ironically, that these technologies are almost always developed *not* by people with MLS degrees makes no difference whatsoever. That these technologies are not "science" either makes no difference, because the blurring in the public mind of technology and science provides a sufficient screen for the library school to continue doing what it has done for many years—provide a good deal of practical technical instruction along with an indoctrination into the belief that librarianship is a profession. All of these factors combine to convey an increasingly pro-innovation bias to students in library schools. They myth being perpetrated is that "newer is better."

Moving on to the Bucher and Strauss notion of "core task" as it applies to segmental conflict within librarianship, it is apparent that the question "What does a librarian do?" has been a thorny one for many years. Much of the difficulty in answering the question stems from the professional/bureaucratic conflict the field is caught up in, as library administrators are, by our definition, librarians, just as catalogers, reference librairans, and book selectors are. I would argue, however, that for the purposes of professionalization of librarianship, the medical paradigm of the doctor-patient relationship looms large in our library schools and our professional literature. Such a paradigm gives special weight to the reference librarian's claim to perform the core task of the field as a whole—providing information directly to users. Parenthetically, I do not wish to leave the impression here that, because I personally am a reference librarian, I am pleading a special status case for reference work; rather, I am trying to develop a more general point. That point is that the recent technological innovations in reference work, most notahbly online bibliographic searching, have had a substantial impact on the public image of librarianship as a whole.

The core task for librarianship in the past has a character that allied librarianship closely with human service occupations such as nursing, medicine and social work. The provision of one-to-one help was first put into practice by Dewey and others to compensate for the complexity of new systems originally designed for self-help.[14] The early theorist of reference service, Samuel Swett Green, developed a rationale for reference[15] that had common intellectual roots with many other late nineteenth-century helping institutions. Giving personal assistance in libraries was an idea of great attraction to an occupation which became available as a career to many educated women at that time, when the institutionalization of charity was a major social force in the United States. In this century, the elaboration of the "core task" nature of reference was undertaken by textbook writers such as Margaret Hutchins[16] and the work of others like Robert Taylor, whose "question negotiation" theory[17] brought reference ideology even closer to that most modern of status occupations, Freudian psychological counseling.[18] A statement made by Verner Clapp in 1966 aptly places this intimate helping image of the reference "core task" at the center of librarianship as a whole:

> Reference work, as we who have labored in its vineyeard have always maintained, is the culmination, the flowering—or, if you will, the reaping and the reward—of library work. For this, from generation to generation, the acquisitions staff has checked dealers' catalogs, bid at auctions, ransacked the bookshops and bookstalls of the world, engaged in inequitable exchanges, and sought out tons of unreadable official publications. For this the bibliophiles collected, and then parted with, their

collections again. For this the never ceasing labors of the cataloging room slowly wrought streamlined order out of incredible chaos, converting an inapprehensible miscellaneity into a comprehensible universe of knowledge. For this the army of encyclopedists, lexicographers, compilers, bibliographers, and indexers selected and anthologized, analyzed and assembled, footnoted and referenced. Of all these labors this, at last, is the payoff. The time may seem to be any time of day. But it is not just any time of day; it is the very moment of truth. In this instant, out of the secret lore, the powerful wisdom that has been entrusted to him, the reference librarian has pronounced an Open Sesame, and the recesses of the library unfold. From among its thousands of volumes and millions of pages shines forth a fact—the information for which an inquirer is waiting at the reference desk, perhaps patiently, perhaps impatiently, and only rarely conscious of the miracle that is being performed on his behalf and which is taking place before his eyes.[19]

It was true, of course, that, even described in such glowing terms, there were grave difficulties with reference service. As several researchers have revealed, the accuracy quotient in reference work is not at all satisfactory.[20] Organizational researchers showed that the work performed by librarians in reference departments was often clerical.[21] Bunge's experiment with nonlibrarians performing reference work provided results that were hardly encouraging to those who felt as Clapp did.[22] But then the technological change of online bibliographic searching came along to allay any doubts librarianship might have had about the primacy of reference.

What online searching did, of course, was to put the reference librarian in a special relationship as intermediary between certain users and a technology which had powerful status association value. I say "certain users" because the cost of the service, both in staff time and in direct money terms, made providing it for all unthinkable. The speed with which online searching was accepted in the field was truly amazing, especially in light of the repeated accusations made by the information science community in the sixties that librarianship was so anti-innovation. Even the barricade of charging for use, thought by some to have had the authority of the Ten Commandments to American librarianship, was quickly brought down with hardly a slingshot volley of a fight. And the reason? In my opinion, it was the status value accompanying the technology that accounts in large measure for the rapid acceptance of online searching. Another reason may have been the desire to protect the performance of the "core task" from being practiced by others—nonlibrarians; thus, the still strong support for the intermediary role among those system designers who closely cater to the interests of reference librarians.[23] Such is one example of the use of a technology for social ends other than the practical end for which it was designed.

This analysis of a technological innovation in the area of a "core task" is meant to suggest that other information technologies may not have such an easy introduction into librarianship unless they can be similarly associated with reference or other broadly recognized core tasks. The transfer of cataloging data through timesharing networks is, of course, widespread by now, but largely due to economics. The professionalization rewards of this innovation are decidely mixed with losses, too, as the change is not highly visible to the public, and catalog librarian jobs are being phased out.[24] Other technologies may not be able to gain a sufficient number of supporters within the occupation to allow the technologies to flourish in libraries, and so they may struggle along, like the audiovisual or microform innovations have, with limited success.

The final ara of the Bucher and Strauss conflict model I will discuss is that concept referred to by them as "spurious unity and public relations." Closely linked with the definition of core task, "spurious unity and public relations" in this context refers to the function that technological change serves librarianship in projecting a particular positive and unified public image. We have seen it referred to in our own literature many times as "the new librarian." Computer terminals, videodiscs, lightpens, and dozens of other devices serve to provide the public mind with a set of related images that leaders in librarianship are very anxious for the public to associate with "librarian." Many, many librarians, of course, have no contact at all with new technologies in their daily work, but that fact can be ignored in the rhetoric of professional image-building.

Besides providing a status association for librarianship to supplant the old spinster stereotype, there is another significant gain for the political leadership of librarianship accomplished by the concentration of attention on technological innovations. That gain is the opportunity to speak for librarianship as if it were a single unified group of 130,000 sophisticated specialists, all highly trained, and basically concerned with the solution of technical problems. Librarianship becomes narrowly defined, in terms of "getting information to people," and the real difficulties we have in complicated sociopolitical decision-making tend not to get discussed in public. We pretend that "getting information to people" is all that there is to it, because that is what we think we know how to do pretty well. But what about the larger issues? What information are we talking about? And which people? These are questions on which it is difficult to reach consensus, and thus are questions that are too often avoided by our profession's political leaders. Some would say that we like technical questions because they are solvable, we dislike philosophical questions because they are not. Consensus on means is easy, consensus on ends probably impossible, and so the leadership takes the easy route.

There is an illusion created, when we skip talking about ends and go straight to discussing means, that we all agree on ends, that that issue has been taken care of. All value debate has been closed off—prematurely, I think. If we are talking about features of a circulation system, for instance, we assume that what we require of any circulation system is generally agreed upon. We have avoided asking whether we need to buy a circulation system more or less than we need more multiple copies, or some other piece of equipment such as a photocopy machine to provide free copies in lieu of loans.[25] We also tend to let our own unspoken values, like "newer is better," to remain unspoken, and thus unexamined.

Because it is difficult to develop consensus on ends, and thus to build political power internally to achieve greater benefits from the lay world, concentration of attention on means—technology—is an attractive strategy for those interested in promoting certain interests of librarianship. Complicated issues like intellectual freedom, or what is just and fair distribution of information in our society, make for long debate, and do not ever lead to final closure, to what some would call "progress." It is much easier to pretend we all agree on what we are collectively about, and get on to the next issue. This, of course, is what we get into when we consider technology first.

Using technology as a tool to create spurious unity and to promote a politically expedient, though inaccurate, public image of librarianship effectively crowds out consideration of our most fundamental problems in the information world. Political, organizational and economic problems do not have technical solutions. And what is worse, technological change brings along with it side impacts in political, organizational and economic spheres. We must know about technology, but if that is all we know, then we are in trouble. We will have no sense of perspective on how best to use it or to judge whether it may cause damage when we use it.

One very serious problem that is nontechnical is that social inequities are developing in terms of accessibility to information. Though we hear much applause in the library press that we are becoming an "information society," our information technologies are helping create a society of information "haves" and information "have-nots." A declining literacy rate is just one sign of this problem. Though there is much touting of the social benefit of decentralization possible with microcomputer technology, we are simultaneously seeing greater centralization develop in larger and larger corporations,[26] centralization that is wiping out some avenues for information dissemination without providing adequate alternative paths.

To summarize in a nutshell what I have presented here concerning a process perspective on librarianship and its relationship to technology, it has been shown with examples that segments of librarianship use technology for their own social ends. Technology in practice is not value-neutral. Adopting one technology may mean forcing out another one. In the area of the recruitment issues to which Bucher and Strauss called attention, we have seen that the new technologies in librarianship may not transform the library schools into halls of science to any significant degree. In relation to the core tasks of librarianship, I have argued that technological adoption of online searching sustained a protectionist attitude, and did not at all indicate a breakthrough in which librarians came around to a more enlightened way of thinking. Technological change also provided a vehicle for groups in librarianship interested in projecting a sense of unity to the lay world—what Bucher and Strauss called "spurious unity and public relations." With all of these points I have been critical of the professionalization movement within librarianship, because I think that movement distracts us from considering more important issues.

I would like to state here that I do believe there is some positive meaning to the term *professional,* if we limit it to the sense that some workers possess special knowledge which they put to use on behalf not of themselves but of the general good as they can best determine it. Acting on behalf of specific others does not necessarily lead to to the general good. There are those like Don Swanson[27] and Paul Zurkowski who would disagree with me on that, and I suppose they have as much right to their ideological position as I have to mine. I do wish, though, that they would not shroud their view in the rhetoric of science, pretending that theirs is a dispassionate and incontrovertible position. I also wish that some librarians would think a bit more critically when they hear technology vendors equate profit and loss with good and bad.

If we librarians are to act in a professional manner in the sense in which I have just described, I believe it is time we take much more seriously the important responsibility we hold in adopting the technologies now rolling out of Silicon Valley workshops. We need to evaluate them carefully before we buy them. We need to make others aware of potential problems we see before others buy them. We urgently need "environmental impact studies" for new information technologies, so as to protect those good parts of our world information environment—like scholarly journals and neighborhood newspapers—that are on the "endangered species" list. Above all, we need to learn more about economics, and learn fast.

REFERENCES

  1. Bucher, Rue, and Strauss, Anselm. "Professions in Process." *American Journal of Sociology* 66(Jan. 1961):325-34.
  2. Dewey, Melvil. "The Profession." *American Library Journal* 1(30 Sept. 1876):5-6.
  3. Flexner, Abraham. "Is Social Work a Profession?" *School and Society* 1(26 June 1915):901-11.
  4. Greenwood, Ernest. "Attributes of a Profession." *Social Work* 2(July 1951):45-55.
  5. For explication of this argument, *see* Roth, Julius A. "Professionalism: The Sociologist's Decoy." *Sociology of Work and Occupations* 1(Feb. 1974):6-23.

6. Bucher and Stauss, "Professions in Process."

7. Ibid., p. 326.

8. Ibid., p. 334.

9. Ibid., pp. 328-30.

10. Ibid., p. 331.

11. Williamson, Charles C. *Training for Library Service: A Report Prepared for the Carnegie Corporation of New York.* New York: Updike, 1923.

12. For a review of this period in American library education, *see* Richardson, John V., Jr. "The Spirit of Inquiry in Library Science." Ph.D. diss., Indiana University, 1978.

13. Bush, Vannevar. "As We May Think." *Atlantic Monthly* 176(July 1945):101-08.

14. Linderman, Winifred B. "History of the Columbia University Libraries." Ph.D. diss., Columbia University, 1959.

15. Green, Samuel Swett. "Personal Relations Between Librarians and Readers." *American Library Journal* 1(Oct. 1876):74-81.

16. Hutchins, Margaret. *Introduction to Reference Work.* Chicago: ALA, 1944.

17. Taylor, Robert S. "Question-Negotiation and Information Seeking in Libraries." *College & Research Libraries* 29(May 1968):178-94. A useful antidote to this theory is provided by Lynch, Mary Jo. "Reference Interviews in Public Libraries." *Library Quarterly* 48(April 1978):11-42.

18. For a general discussion of the ideological underpinnings of the service philosophy which librarianship shares with other occupations, *see* Halmos, Paul. *The Personal Service Society.* New York: Schocken Books, 1970.

19. Clapp, Verner W. "Some Thoughts on the Present Status and Future Prospects of Reference Work." In *The Present Status and Future Prospects of Reference/Information Service* (Proceedings of the Conference held at the School of Library Service, Columbia University, March 30—April 1, 1966), edited by Winifred B. Linderman, p. 1. Chicago: ALA, 1967.

20. For a useful review, *see* Lancaster, F. Wilfrid. *The Measurement and Evaluation of Library Services.* Washington, D.C.: Information Resources Press, 1977, pp. 91-109.

21. *See* Lawson, Venable. "Reference Service in University Libraries: Two Case Studies." Ph.D. diss., Columbia University, 1970; and Jestes, E.C., and Laird, W.D. "A Time Study of General Reference Work in a University Library." *Research in Librarianship* 2(1968):9-16.

22. Bunge, Charles. "Professional Education and Reference Efficiency." Ph.D. diss., University of Illinois at Urbana-Champaign, 1967.

23. Summit, Roger. "Popular Illusions Relating to the Costs of Online Services." Address delivered at the ALA/RASD/MARS program, "Cooperation: Facilitating Access to Online Information Services," 29 June 1980, New York.

24. Gorman, Michael. "Technical Services in an Automated Library." In *The Role of the Library in an Electronic Society* (Proceedings of the 1979 Clinic on Library Applications of Data Processing), edited by F. Wilfrid Lancaster, pp. 48-59. Urbana-Champaign: University of Illinois Graduate School of Library Science, 1980.

25. For a discussion of this general issue, which uses this specific example, *see* Raffel, Jeffrey A. "From Economic to Political Analysis of Library Decision Making." *College & Research Libraries* 35(Nov. 1974):412-23.

26. For an untangling of this seeming paradox, *see* Simon, Herbert A. "The Consequences of Computers for Centralization and Decentralization." In *The Computer Age: A Twenty-Year View,* edited by Michael L. Dertouzos and Joel Moses, pp. 212-28. Cambridge, Mass.: MIT Press, 1979.

27. Swanson, Don R. "Information Retrieval as a Trial-and-Error Process." *Library Quarterly* 47(April 1977):145.

CONTRIBUTORS

J.L. DIVILBISS is Associate Professor in the Graduate School of Library and Information Science and Principal Research Engineer in the Coordinated Science Laboratory at the University of Illinois at Urbana-Champaign. He received his Ph.D. in electrical engineering from the University of Illinois and worked at Bell Telephone Laboratories before returning to head the engineering team for the Illiac III computer. He currently teaches courses in library automation, systems analysis, and telecommunications.

HOWARD FOSDICK is an independent consultant in the Chicago area and was previously a designer of online information systems for GTE Automatic Electric Laboratories in Northlake, Illinois. He holds master's degrees in library science from the University of Illinois and in computer science from Northern Illinois University. His papers have been published in journals in both fields. He is author of *Computer Basics for Librarians and Information Scientists* and *Structured PL/I Programming: For Textual and Library Processing.*

DAVID R. HOYT is a Technical Information Specialist with Technical Information Systems in the Science and Education Administration of the U.S. Department of Agriculture, where he is responsible for education, training, and public outreach. He holds a master's degree in library science from Indiana University and a master's degree in the history of ideas from Johns Hopkins University. He was previously a reference librarian and database searcher at the National Agricultural Library.

JEROME K. MILLER is a member of the faculty of the Graduate School of Library and Information Science at the University of Illinois at Urbana-Champaign. He received an Ed.D. in educational media from the University of Colorado. He is the author of several publications dealing with copyright, including two books: *Applying the New Copyright Law: A Guide for Educators and Librarians* and *U.S. Copyright Documents: An Annotated Collection for Use by Educators and Librarians.*

BRIAN NIELSEN is Head of the Reference Department of Northwestern University Library. He is a doctoral candidate in library science at the University of North Carolina at Chapel Hill and has held various positions in the library there, most recently that of Assistant Undergraduate Librarian for Reference and Instruction. He received the "best paper" award at the 1980 National Online Information Meeting for his paper

"Online Bibliographic Searching and the Deprofessionalization of Librarianship."

W. DAVID PENNIMAN is Vice-President, Planning and Research and Director, Development Division, OCLC Online Computer Library Center, Inc. He received a Ph.D. in communication theory from Ohio State University. He was previously Associate Manager of the Information Systems Section at Battelle Columbus Laboratories and Manager of the Research Department at OCLC. His experience in the field of information systems research and development has included involvement in the areas of human factors, human-computer interaction, computer networks, and information system evaluation. THOMAS B. HICKEY and HOWARD TURTLE, both senior research scientists at the OCLC Online Computer Library Center, Inc., helped with the preparation of the paper.

PETER B. SCHIPMA is Manager, Information Sciences at the IIT Research Institute. He holds both a B.S. in physics and an M.S. in science information from the Illinois Institute of Technology. He has been with IITRI since 1967, where he has managed several research contracts and grants in the information sciences area. His responsibilities include serving as Manager of the Computer Search Center at IITRI and as Director of the Computer Support Center of the National Cancer Institute International Cancer Research Data Bank Program.

LINDA C. SMITH is a member of the faculty of the Graduate School of Library and Information Science at the University of Illinois at Urbana-Champaign. She received a Ph.D. from the School of Information Studies at Syracuse University. Her fields of interest include information retrieval, library automation, and science reference service.

RICHARD H. VEITH is currently a consultant with Logica, Inc., New York, working on videotex and teletext projects. He received his Ph.D. in information studies from Syracuse University, and an M.A. in radio and television from San Francisco State University. He has previously been an information systems specialist with Informatics, Inc. and a lecturer at San Francisco State University. His publications include a book on two-way cable television in the United States, and a forthcoming book on international computer networks.

RONALD L. WIGINGTON is Director of Research and Development for Chemical Abstracts Service. He received a Ph.D. in electrical engineering from University of Kansas, and graduated from the Advanced Management Program of the Harvard Business School. His experience includes work in computer technology and electronics research and development in the Department of Defense and the Bell Telephone Laboratories. He has participated in a wide variety of advisory boards and study panels, and is the author of numerous papers on computer techniques, library topics, and information systems.

LAWRENCE A. WOODS is Head of Research and Development for Purdue University Libraries. He holds a master's degree in library science from Simmons College. Before coming to Purdue he was Chief of Systems Design and Maintenance for Dartmouth College Libraries. He has recently organized and chaired two workshops on Microcomputers in Libraries for the ASIS Special Interest Group on Library Automation and Networks, and he is also preparing a book on that topic.

INDEX